CHILDREN'S DRAWINGS OF THE HUMAN FIGURE

Children's Drawings of the Human Figure

Maureen V. Cox

Department of Psychology, University of York, UK

 LAWRENCE ERLBAUM ASSOCIATES, PUBLISHERS
Hove (UK)   Hillsdale (USA)

Lawrence Erlbaum Associates Ltd., Publishers
27 Palmeira Mansions
Church Road
Hove
East Sussex, BN3 2FA
UK

British Library Cataloguing in Publication Data

Cox, M.V.
  Children's Drawings of the Human Figure.
  — (Essays in Developmental Psychology,
  ISSN 0959–3977)
  I. Title II. Series
  155.4

  ISBN 0–86377–268–4

Cover by Joyce Chester
Typeset by J&L Composition Ltd., Filey, North Yorkshire
Printed and bound in the United Kingdom
by Redwood Books, Trowbridge

Contents

Acknowledgements

My thanks go to a number of colleagues and students who have helped in the preparation of this book by supplying references, figures and data: Dr Rüvide Bayraktar (Fig. 7.2), Dr Poonam Batra (Fig. 7.9), Elsbeth Court, Dr Alyson Davis (Fig. 6.2), Dr Jan Deręgowski, Aileen Hope (Fig. 7.3), Glyn Jarvis, Professor Paul Light and Ruth Sittow (Fig. 6.1), Dr Karen Littleton, Dr John Matthews (Figs 1.2 and 1.4), Dr Karen Pfeffer (Figs 7.7 and 7.8), Ruth Stoker, Helen Windybank (Fig. 2.6), Rachel Moore, Stephanie Osmond, John Stone, Dr John Willats (Figs 1.5 and 1.6) and Professor Brent Wilson (Figs 7.10 and 7.11). I am also indebted to Professor Peter Bryant, Professor George Butterworth and Dr James Thomson for their useful comments on the first draft of the manuscript. Finally, my thanks go to Dr Tony Wootton for his meticulous reading of the manuscript and his generosity in giving up his time to discuss the ideas and issues contained in it.

A Note on Gender

In the interests of equality, the gender of the children in this book alternates from one chapter to the next.

Introduction

As part of the growing interest in child study during the nineteenth century, a number of eminent people, Charles Darwin (1877) among them, included children's drawings in their observations and investigations. One of the first published papers devoted solely to children's artwork was Ebenezer Cooke's 'Our art teaching and child nature' (1886). This was followed by the now more famous monograph *L'Arte dei Bambini* by Corrado Ricci (1887). Ricci is supposed to have been inspired by the graffiti drawings he saw in a doorway as he sheltered from the rain. He was particularly struck by what seemed to be developmental differences between the lower figures, which he presumed to have been drawn by younger children, and the upper ones drawn by older children. Ricci's subsequent collection of children's drawings is one of the earliest to have been published and his observations of the development of the human figure in children's drawings remain important over a century later.

The human figure is one of the first topics to be drawn by young children and also remains one of the most frequently chosen topics (Maitland, 1895; Märtin, 1939; McCarty, 1924). In a study of 864 children's drawings, Lark-Horovitz, Barnhart and Sills (1939) found that the human figure was not only the most frequently drawn topic but also that drawings of humans in their surroundings decreased during childhood, whereas drawings of the human figure alone increased; in particular, the incidence of head portraits increased in early adolescence.

Children's earliest recognisable human figure drawings are very minimal and consist of what appears to be a head set upon two legs; there may also be facial features, hair and arms. With increasing age, the child adds more

1

details, one of the most important for the construction of the figure being the introduction of a torso as a distinct and separate item. In a very large study of human figure drawings, Partridge (1902) collected figures from 200 children at each age level from 4 to 10 years and made a record of the typical ages at which children drew different parts of the body. She found that the addition of details carries on until about the age of 12 years, when children begin to be more interested in only the head of the figure and in considerations of proportion, shading and perspective.

The observation that the sequential addition of details and the increasingly realistic proportions of the body parts are correlated with age during childhood (Schuyten, 1904), and even more so with mental age (Rouma, 1913), led to the use of human figure drawings as a test of children's intelligence or intellectual maturity. One of the earliest attempts was made by Schuyten (1904), but the more successful and well-known Draw-a-Man Test was devised by Goodenough (1926) and was later revised by Harris (1963). A more recent test of mental maturity based on developmental items—the Draw-a-Person Test—has been devised by Koppitz (1968).

One of the earliest researchers to detail a developmental sequence in children's drawing of the human figure was Rouma (1913), who based his stages not on any statistical analyses but on his very careful observations of normal children from kindergarten up to the age of 11 years, as well as some children with learning difficulties. Although other researchers (e.g. Burt, 1921; Luquet, 1913) have also postulated developmental stages in drawing, Rouma (1913) did this specifically in relation to children's drawings of the human figure rather than drawing in general. As will become evident in the following chapters, the sequence of Rouma's stages has been largely borne out by subsequent studies of children's human figure drawing:

I. The preliminary stage.
   1. Adaptation of the hand to the instrument.
   2. The child gives a definite name to the incoherent lines which he traces.
   3. The child announces in advance that which he intends to represent.
   4. The child sees a resemblance between the lines obtained by chance and certain objects.
II. Evolution of the representation of the human figure.
   1. First tentative attempts at representation, similar to the preliminary stages.
   2. The "tadpole" stage.
   3. Transitional stage.
   4. Complete representation of the human figure as seen in full face.

5. Transitional stage between full face and profile.
6. The profile.

Since this general pattern of development is so very characteristic of children's drawing, it is perhaps not surprising that psychologists and educationists have found the idea of a non-verbal task—the drawing of the human figure—very useful in assessing a child's developmental level when that child may have difficulties understanding a language-based task. Indeed, the task has been advocated as a useful means of making comparisons across different cultures without the difficulties involved when using a language-biased or culturally biased test.

As well as using children's drawings to diagnose their level of intelligence or intellectual maturity, researchers and practitioners have also used drawings as a basis for the diagnosis of personality disorders or emotional maladjustment (Koppitz, 1968; Machover, 1949). Since individual children's drawings are so distinctive and adults can recognise the style of children as young as 5 years of age (Hartley, Somerville, von Cziesch Jensen, & Eliefja, 1982), it is perhaps not unreasonable to expect these drawings to reflect something of the social-emotional as well as the intellectual side of a child's nature.

Many of the claims regarding the significance of a child's drawing in this respect are based on psychoanalytic or quasi-psychoanalytic theory, which assumes that the inclusion or omission of certain body parts, as well as the way they are drawn, is symbolic of the child's feelings, fears and anxieties. The validity of two particular approaches—those of Machover (1949) and Koppitz (1968)—will be considered in this book. So, too, will a more recent experimental approach to the understanding of the typical charac-teristics of many children's drawings. This approach seeks to test what many may regard as more mundane, though perhaps more parsimonious, hypotheses for the phenomena in question. For example, in contrast to the claim that children draw disproportionately large heads on their figures because the head is the most important and symbolic part of a person, the experimentalists have suggested that the large heads may be a result of the problem of planning the relative sizes of different body parts: Since the head of the figure is normally the first item to be drawn, it may take up a disproportionate amount of the available space, but also the child may deliberately draw a large outline because he plans to include the facial details within it.

In the earlier part of the twentieth century, drawing appeared as a timetabled subject in the school curriculum, although it was actually available mainly to boys while girls were doing needlework. Given this difference in the time and opportunity for drawing, it is perhaps not surprising that the boys were considered more able than the girls. I shall evaluate the present-day evidence pertaining to this claim as well as that which has a bearing on the differences or preferences in the way that boys and girls draw. Furthermore, I shall consider the ways that both boys and girls depict male and female figures in their drawings, i.e. the ways in which figures can be identified as male or female.

Research on children's drawings of the human figure has not been solely descriptive, nor has it been carried out to serve only a diagnostic function; even in the early years of work in this area, researchers such as Ricci (1887) were addressing the question of why children draw figures in the way they do. My main purpose in writing this book is to describe and explain on the basis of the research currently available the development of children's human figure drawing, beginning even before the first figures become recognisable. The ideas discussed, however, pertain not only to human figure drawings but encompass the activity of drawing in general, and in many cases also have wider implications for our representational skills, children's and adults' alike.

It has been assumed that when children first apply pencil to paper they are not intending to be representational at all but are, at first, simply enjoying the movement and then, later, the various marks that they produce (Bender, 1938; Harris, 1963; Kellogg, 1969). Kellogg, who set out to document the precursors to representational drawing among a collection of nearly one million children's drawings, claimed that young children are striving towards the production of aesthetically well-balanced forms and have no intention of trying to represent objects or events. More recently, however, Matthews (1984) and Wolf and Perry (1988) have challenged this view and have argued that the traditional distinction made between the earlier pre-representational or pre-schematic stage and the later representational stage is too simple. I shall present some of their evidence, which indicates that scribblers do at least sometimes represent in their drawings the actions and events occurring in their world.

One of the earliest recognisable forms which children produce, the tadpole figure, has attracted a number of different explanations. These range from the claim that the child simply copies the tadpole form from other drawers to the claim that the child constructs his own internal model of the figure which he then uses to guide the drawing (Luquet, 1913; 1927; Piaget & Inhelder, 1956). Not all researchers have agreed on the nature of such a mental model, nor on the extent to which children can or do use it directly to inform the drawing. Whereas some assume a more or less direct mapping from the internal model to the figure on the page, others believe that other processes and difficulties intervene; for example, the child may not be able to recall all the different elements of the figure (Freeman, 1975; 1980), he may choose not to draw them all (Golomb, 1981), he may not have differentiated all of the body parts (Arnheim,

1974), or he may not have devised ways of graphically representing all of them.

Since most children are not taught how to draw but appear to discover or invent recognisable schemas for themselves, they are faced with the problem of what kinds of marks and shapes they should use. This problem has been addressed by Willats (1985; 1987), who argues that the child identifies the salient shape of each element to be drawn—for instance, the bulkiness of the head or the elongated shape of a leg or an arm—and then selects from his repertoire the lines or shapes which would be most appropriate to stand for each element. In order to elaborate the figure, he will need to extend this repertoire. The way that children draw the various elements of their figures changes in a systematic way in most Western cultures; for example, very young children use single lines to depict the limbs of their figures, older children depict the limbs as "tubes", and yet older children combine body parts, such as the arms and the torso, with a continuous outline.

Children's human figure drawings appear to become more realistic as they add more and more details to them. Even so, although their figures are more elaborate compared with those of younger children, they are none the less typically presented in a rather "stiff" pose and in a frontal or canonical orientation. The figures are drawn so that all the body parts are clearly displayed and do not overlap each other; in fact, as Goodnow (1977) argues, they seem to be following the rule "each to its own space".These figures are not visually realistic in the sense of being photographically correct. Indeed, it has been argued that the young child is more concerned to display what he knows about the object rather than what he sees, a concern referred to as *intellectual realism* by Luquet (1913; 1927). Very often, this concern results in an impossible view of the figure.

A shift from intellectual realism towards *visual realism* comes about when the child, at about the age of 7–8 years, begins to develop projective concepts of space and to adopt a particular point of view *vis-à-vis* the figure (Piaget & Inhelder, 1956). He becomes concerned to draw only those parts of a figure that could be seen from a certain viewpoint and to omit those that would be occluded. His outline of the figure or of a particular part of it is used as an occluding contour which outlines, say, an arm against the background of the torso as a particular observer would see it from a specific viewpoint. The flexibility of the figure afforded by the use of a contouring outline rather than segmented parts is evident in the older child's drawings of profile figures engaged in various kinds of activity. The impetus for such a shift towards visual realism is unclear. However, since it is not universal and it has not been a hallmark of adult art throughout historical time, it is likely that children are influenced by the prevailing culture which surrounds them and at present this is replete with photographic images in books, magazines, television advertising, and so on.

Since much of the research on drawing has been conducted by Western researchers, with Western assumptions and in Western cultures, most of the published work reflects this bias. It has become almost axiomatic that in Western cultures children progress from a period of scribbling to the production of tadpole forms and then on to conventional forms, at first composed of segmented body parts and then later of more contoured and integrated sections. Despite the claim by Kellogg (1969) that there are cultural similarities among children's drawings, in non-Western cultures we see very different styles and different patterns of progress. In cultures in which children—and indeed adults—have had no previous opportunity to draw, they may spend little or no time in scribbling before attempting a representational drawing. Their human figure drawings often appear visually unrealistic and often almost unrecognisable. For example, the head may be drawn as a small blob with no facial features at all or it may appear at the top of a vertical "string" as an item separate from the facial features which are "listed" below it. Thus, the facial features are not necessarily encompassed by a facial boundary, nor are the features of the torso enclosed by a contour representing the "body" of the figure. I shall review some of the cross-cultural data, past and present, which demonstrate the diversity of styles worldwide. This diversity leads us to question a long-held assumption, implicit in much research, that "West is best" and that other forms of representation are necessarily inferior. It also leads us to question the universality of the cognitive explanations for the way that children draw, in particular the idea that children everywhere conceptualise the human figure in a similar way and then transfer that image or concept directly onto the page. Furthermore, a practical implication is that the use of drawings as a culture-free way of comparing children's development in different societies is untenable.

1 The Meaning of the Marks

Scribbling

Long before they produce any recognisable pictures, children in most Western cultures make marks on a piece of paper with a crayon or pencil. These first scribbles appear around the age of 12 months, although individual children will be more or less advanced depending on the availability of materials, parental encouragement, and so on. The earliest marks are often rather tentative, even though there are some children who stab at the page with their pencil. Either way, the movements are generally unplanned and uncontrolled. These early attempts may in fact be imitations of the adult's hand movements as Major (1906) suggested. His son, "R", seemed reluctant or unable to attempt the task at all without his father's demonstrations.

It has been argued by Bender (1938) and Harris (1963, p. 228), for example, that children enjoy scribbling primarily because of the motor movement it involves. While not denying that this enjoyment of movement is important, it is clear that the production of marks on the page is also of great interest to the child. If children are given a pencil-like implement that does not leave a mark, they quickly lose interest in the activity (Gibson & Yonas, cited in Gibson, 1969, pp. 446–447).

As children gain more experience with the pencil, their scribbles become more distinct and their repertoire more varied. In fact, among her collection of approximately one million children's drawings, Kellogg (1969) identified 20 different basic scribbles. She claimed that these scribbles are the basic units which are combined and recombined into

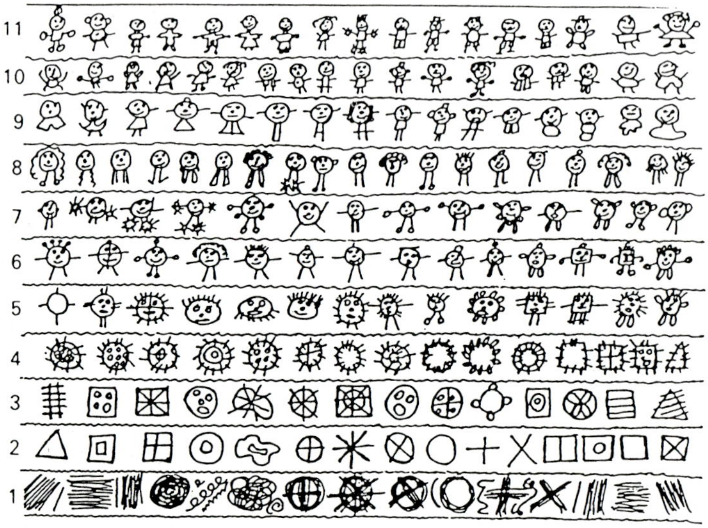

FIG. 1.1   Kellogg (1969) suggested that the child's human figure drawings evolve from earlier scribbles and patterns.

progressively more complex forms such as *diagrams* (crosses, rectangles, etc.), *combines* (units of two diagrams), *aggregates* (units of three or more diagrams), etc. (see Fig. 1.1). Kellogg argued that there is no indication that these scribbles or designs are meant to be representational, in the sense of "standing for" something in the real world. Indeed, she maintained that the process of combining and recombining the scribble formations is not determined at all by the visual world, but by the child's sense of aesthetic balance, which in itself Kellogg takes to be innate and universal. When the child eventually does come to make representational drawings, she calls on these non-representational forms in her repertoire, and so her human figure drawings owe more to those earlier forms than they do to the visual characteristics of real people. The *mandalas* (see level 3 in Fig. 1.1) and *sun schemas* (level 4) in particular are the basic designs which children typically employ in their first attempts at human figure drawing.

An Evaluation of Kellogg's Theory

This "building block" notion of the development of drawing emerged from Kellogg's study of her vast collection of children's spontaneous drawings. Although, from other data too, there does appear to be an age-related shift from early uncontrolled scribbles through more distinct forms to later representational forms ($r = 0.85$: Cox & Parkin, 1986), there is little evidence that *all* children necessarily go through the same specific and detailed sequence of steps proposed by Kellogg. In fact, Kellogg herself, as Golomb (1981) points out, reports a very low incidence of forms such as the *mandala* and the *sun schema*, which are supposed to be important precursors to the child's construction of the human figure (the highest percentage of the occurrence of the mandala was 9.62 in the age range 24–30 months and the highest percentage of the occurrence of the sun schema was 4.1 in the age range 49–54 months). Furthermore, the sun schemas and the first human figures appear at the same time (mean age 3 years 7 months), a finding which contradicts the notion of a stage-like progression.

When Golomb (1981) and her co-worker, Linda Whitaker, analysed the scribbles produced by their own 2- to 4-year-olds, they encountered a number of problems in classifying the scribbles according to Kellogg's 20 basic categories. The main difficulty concerned inter-rater reliability, which was extremely low when the raters scored the finished drawings. It rose to 70%, however, when the raters watched the whole process of the child's scribbling, but still only two broad categories of scribble could be identified: (1) whirls, loops and circles and (2) multiple densely patterned parallel lines.

There is also other evidence which casts doubt on Kellogg's stage hypothesis. This comes from a number of studies (e.g. Alland, 1983; Gardner, 1980; Harris, 1971; Millar, 1975) in which children or adults have, for various reasons, been previously deprived of the opportunity to draw. Despite this, they quickly move from scribbling "exercises" to drawing recognisable human forms without passing through the stages suggested by Kellogg. Golomb (1981) also notes that 39% of her 2-year-old scribblers and 80% of her 3-year-old scribblers produced a representational picture on request, or dictation by the experimenter, even though they had not progressed through Kellogg's sequence of supposedly pre-requisite stages.

Early Non-pictorial Representations

In general, then, the evidence does not support Kellogg's building-block notion of the development from scribbles to recognisable representational forms. But we are still left with the question of what is going on at the scribbling stage. It could be that children are simply developing an understanding of the relationship between their motor movements and the production of the marks on the page and are then deliberately attempting to vary the kinds of marks they produce. While not seeking to deny the importance of these particular functions or outcomes of the scribbling process, there is evidence which none the less points to a representational intention on the part of the scribbling child.

Although it may seem curious to try to advocate such a position when the young child's scribbles appear, almost by definition, to be *non*-representational, children do use forms of representation which are non-pictorial and which are not detectable if we consider only the final product of the child's scribbling exercise. Indeed, Freeman (1972) has pointed out that an analysis based solely on children's completed drawings or scribbles may give us an incomplete or even a distorted view of their meaning. Thus, if we concentrate on the final product, we may well try to interpret the scribble in terms of its visual likeness to a particular object, and in nearly all cases we shall judge there to be little or no similarity and conclude that the scribble is therefore non-representational. If, on the other hand, we consider the *process* of the drawing exercise as well as the final product, we may discover that the child is attempting to represent objects or events even though this is not done in a conventional, pictorial sense. Given that very young children from as early as 12 or 13 months (Cox, 1991) are routinely engaged in representational or symbolic behaviour, through language and pretend play for example, it would be extraordinary to find no representation whatsoever in their drawing activities.

The main evidence that non-pictorial representation is a part of the scribbling child's activity comes from the work of Wolf and Perry (1988) and Matthews (1984). Wolf and Perry note that children, beginning at about the age of 12–14 months, will use the drawing materials themselves to symbolise objects, relationships or events. In these *object-based representations*, as these researchers call them, a child may, for example, roll up a crayon inside a piece of paper and call out "hot dog". Also, in the second year, a child may demonstrate *gestural representations*, again using the drawing materials themselves: One child, for instance, "hopped" a pen across the page, saying "bunny", and created a trail of dotted footprints. The reference to gestural representations endorses Vygotsky's (1978, p. 107) assertion that, "In general, we are inclined to view children's first drawings and scribbles rather as gestures than as drawing in the true sense of the word."

Matthews (1984) gives similar examples of what he calls *action representations*. Ben, aged 2 years 1 month, rotates his paintbrush on the page producing a continuous series of overlapping spirals (see Fig. 1.2) and describes what is going on: ". . . it's going round the corner. It's going round the corner. It's gone now." Matthews argues that Ben is describing the movement of an imaginary object, probably a car, which is symbolised by the tip of the brush. The action is taking place in three-dimensional space and Ben's commentary draws attention to some of the qualities of the movements within that space (its direction round a corner and its eventual disappearance). It is interesting that Ben's announcement that the car had disappeared seemed to be made when the line had become

FIG. 1.2 Ben (aged 2 years 1 month): ". . . it's going round the corner. It's going round the corner. It's gone now." (Reproduced with the permission of Dr John Matthews.)

submerged under layers of paint and was no longer clearly visible; this suggests that the marks on the page are not merely a by-product of the child's activity but can guide and alter his interpretation of his actions.

Wolf and Perry (1988) argue that these early representational systems commit meaning to paper, although not in the usual pictorial sense, and that they may be important in laying a foundation for later and more conventionally pictorial systems of representation. From about the age of 20 months, according to Wolf and Perry, children are able to make separate marks for objects or parts of objects. So, for example, they may make a mark for a head, another for a tummy, and further marks for the feet of a person. In this *point-plot representation*, the children are recording the existence of different items, their number (one head, two feet, etc.) and often their spatial position (head at the top of the figure, tummy lower down and feet at the bottom). In this system, there is the first indication that the marks themselves rather than the child's attendant behaviour (sounds, gestures, etc.) are carrying the meaning, even though there is little or no visual correspondence between the shape of the marks and the shape of the items they stand for.

Fortuitous Realism

Between about 18 and 30 months, children begin to monitor the marks they create on the page and may see pictures in them, such as "a pelican kissing a seal" or "noodles in soup", to use two examples given by Wolf and Perry. These productions are, of course, accidental; the child has no plan or prior intention regarding the particular subject matter of the drawing. This ability to recognise something in the scribbles was also noted by Luquet (1913; 1927) and referred to aptly as *fortuitous realism*.

One of the developments which may in fact promote children's tendencies to notice things in their scribbles is their developing control over the pencil and their ability to make loopy scribbles which bound an enclosed space. The loopy or spiral scribbles become more controlled until the child can curtail the spiral and join the ends to make a rough circle (Bender, 1938; Piaget & Inhelder, 1956). Arnheim (1974) has pointed out the special significance that a circle seems to have: It bounds an inside area which attains a solid-looking quality and is readily recognised as a figure set against a background. In fact, Arnheim regards the circle as one of the most primary percepts. Some children may be able to add further appropriate details to their scribbles once a particular object has been recognised. One child aged 2 years 10 months, expressed surprise after she had drawn a closed shape, saying "Look! That's a bird!" (Cox, 1991). She then went on to add a dot, saying "He needs an eye", and a number of lines, saying "They have legs, don't they? Five legs!" (see Fig. 1.3).

FIG. 1.3   *A bird*, drawn by Amy, aged 2 years 10 months. (Reproduced with the permission of Harvester Wheatsheaf.)

Pictorial Representation

Towards the end of their second year, children begin to construct forms on the page which have more visual-spatial correspondence to the objects they are intending to represent. Matthews (1984) calls this *figurative representation*. There may, nevertheless, still be some discrepancy between the children's intentions and what they actually produce and, although they may not set out to draw a particular object, they may change their minds in mid-drawing if the marks on the page remind them of something else. Soon, however, children develop more reliable means of representing visual-spatial information about objects, which also enables others to recognise readily what they have drawn.

Wolf and Perry (1988) are at pains to emphasise that although there is some developmental emergence of the different ways of representing

FIG. 1.4 *Someone washing*, drawn by Ben, aged 3 years 1 month. (Reproduced with the permission of Dr John Matthews.)

objects on a page, the systems should not be seen as mutually exclusive and stage-like, since children continue to use and to develop a number of different systems, a point also endorsed by Matthews (1984). A child may in fact combine different systems in the same drawing. Ben, at nearly 3 years 1 month, drew "someone washing" (see Fig. 1.4). There is evidence of figurative representation (to use Matthews' term) in the drawing of the tap and the two arms of a person reaching into the basin. There is also evidence of action representation in the continuous rotations of the paintbrush, representing the swirling of the hands in the water. Combinations of different systems are also used by much older children who represent the movement or trajectory of a person or a vehicle by single or dotted lines.

Although children develop a variety of graphic representational systems and may use them in combination, it is nevertheless the *visual-pictorial* which becomes dominant in the sense that the child intends to capture some visual aspect of the object—its shape, the proportions and spatial arrangement of its constituent parts, etc. Indeed, Golomb (1981) argues that the main concern of the child who makes the transition from scribbles to representational forms is with *visual likeness to the object*.

If the child's intention is to capture some visual likeness to the real object, then the problem becomes one of finding appropriate pictorial ways of suggesting various properties of the object. This process has been described as a "search for equivalents" (Goodnow, 1977) and also as a "search for meaning and likeness" (Golomb, 1981), based on an idea put forward earlier by Arnheim (1974). Children may already have experimented with closed shapes and these, as Arnheim has noted, seem to be universally recognised as depictions of objects against their background; since blind subjects also recognise raised outline drawings in this way, it is likely that the notion of lines standing for surface or contour edges of objects can be derived from both the visual and the tactile channels of perception (Kennedy, 1983; Millar, 1975). Many children, then, will already have in their repertoire some potential candidates for use in their representational drawings—in particular, they will probably be able to draw closed forms as well as single lines. But, whether these forms have already been practised or not, the important point, as Golomb (1981) insists, is that it is the children's representational *intentions* which determine the choice of forms and these intentions usually concern the urge to represent something of the visual characteristics of objects in the real world.

Denotation Systems

Willats (1985; 1987) has formalised the way he thinks that children, and indeed adults, go about the task of selecting or, if necessary, inventing graphic forms in order to capture some visual correspondence between the drawing and the real object.

Many of the objects we wish to draw are volumetric, i.e. they exist in three dimensions in the real world. However, they are not all the same shape. The head of a person, for example, is a fairly bulky object extending more or less equally in all three dimensions of space. The palm of the hand is slab-like, extending mainly in two dimensions. A leg is not bulky like a head, nor is it slab-like; it is a long thing markedly extending in only one dimension. Thus, we can describe these three-dimensional body parts in terms of their salient dimensions.

Willats uses a formal index of extension for this purpose, with the figure "3" indicating a three-dimensional object and then three subscripts indicating its extension, or relative lack of extension, in each of the three spatial dimensions. Thus, a bulky, spherical head is written as 3_{111}, a flat, slab-like hand as 3_{110} and a leg as 3_{100}. The figure "3", then, indicates that these body parts or *scene primitives*, as Willats calls them, are three-dimensional.

We do not always wish to draw three-dimensional body parts, however. For example, even though an eye is a three-dimensional object, the part that we draw in a figure drawing is a two-dimensional surface, and Willats uses a figure "2" to denote this two-dimensional scene primitive. Similarly, the slit of the mouth is like a line and is denoted by a figure "1" and the point-like pupils of the eyes by a "0". It seems that Willats does not necessarily intend these particular indices to be fixed, but has based them on an intuitive notion of how people might think about the properties of different body parts. Of course, we do not know whether children or adults do think of them in this way, nor whether their conceptualisation of different body parts is universal (this issue will be discussed later in Chapters 7 and 8).

In order to represent the various body parts in a drawing, we have to select the appropriate graphic forms which will best denote them. And we choose from a number of picture primitives, i.e. dots, lines and regions. In the same way that the scene primitives are each given an index of extension by Willats, so too are the picture primitives: a dot is 0, a line is 1, and regions are either more or less circular (2_{11}) or elongated (2_{10}).

Since, on a page, we cannot represent a three-dimensional volume by three-dimensional means, the best thing to do would be to choose a picture primitive with the highest possible dimensional index. Thus, we should use a region, rather than a dot or a line, to denote a volume. If it is, in fact, a surface we are depicting, then indeed a region would be the most appropriate. Similarly, a line would be best to depict something which is linear in the real scene and a dot something which is dot-like.

Using this system, Willats suggests how a young child might select suitable picture primitives to stand for the various body parts of the human figure. He presumes that although the child already has in her graphic repertoire dots, lines and circular regions, she cannot alter the shape of the regions, either because she lacks the motor control (Olivier, 1974) or because "the ability to handle the symbolism involved in using two different kinds of two-dimensional primitives has not yet developed" (Willats, 1985, p. 94). Whatever the reason, she basically has only dots, single lines and one standard, roughly circular region at her disposal, although as Willats says, she can alter the size of the region if not its shape. Now, as we know, very young children draw tadpole forms (see Chapter 2): a very simple form is a head with facial features and two arms and two legs. When drawing the tadpole, then, the young child chooses a region to represent the bulky head of the figure and lines to represent the long limbs of the figure. In the example that Willats uses to illustrate the system (see Fig. 1.5), the child also uses small regions to represent the eyes. We can see, then, how the child selects the most appropriate picture primitives in her repertoire which will map onto her mental descriptions of the body parts of a real person.

Willats argues that with such a small repertoire of picture primitives available to the child, there would be considerable ambiguity regarding the identity of different body parts if she used, say, a standard region to represent each one of them. He argues that the introduction or discovery

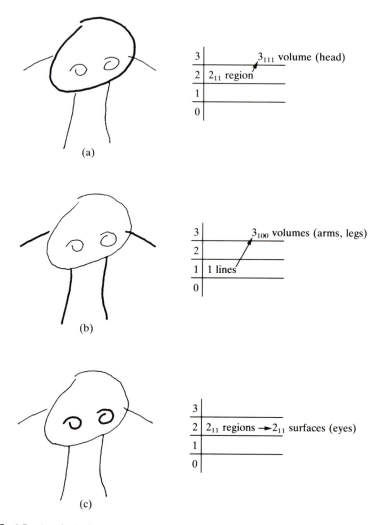

FIG. 1.5   A tadpole figure, showing suggested denotation systems for the various parts.

of new picture primitives is what enables the child to add new features to her figures. Giving an example of a more detailed tadpole figure, Willats shows how the child uses a region for the head and lines for the limbs, but now uses dots for the eyes (see Fig. 1.6). He argues that this introduction of dots releases the region to be used for other things. This argument is flawed, however. There is no reason why the child should not have used dots for eyes in the first place, since dots are already in the repertoire of most children at this stage. Having chosen regions, however, there is no

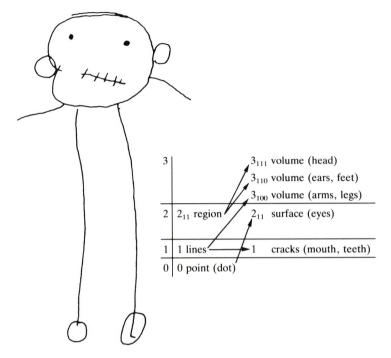

The figure includes the following labels:

3		3_{111} volume (head)
		3_{110} volume (ears, feet)
		3_{100} volume (arms, legs)
2	2_{11} region	2_{11} surface (eyes)
1	1 lines	1 cracks (mouth, teeth)
0	0 point (dot)	

FIG. 1.6   Willats' analysis of a child's drawing of a man.

reason why she should not continue using regions for eyes. To start with, it would not preclude their use for feet or ears, nor indeed for other body parts. And, further, a figure made up of regions would not necessarily be ambiguous, since the spatial arrangement of the various parts of a figure indicates what each part is meant to be. Thus, Willats' general argument that the child can only add more body parts if she can go on finding more ways of representing them is not acceptable.

A claim which seems more reasonable, however, is one regarding the shift towards using regions instead of lines for the limbs of the figure. By doing this, the child makes the drawing more realistic; in contrast to the stick-like limbs of the early figures, the "tubes" of the later ones outline the shape of real legs projected onto the visual field. Thus the argument here is that the child moves towards making the parts of the figure more visually realistic, an argument also put forward by Fenson (1985). In a sample of 454 human figure drawings (see Chapter 3), I found that 84% of the 60 tadpole-drawers and 14 transitional-drawers who added arms to their figures drew them as single lines and only 16% drew them as enclosed regions; in contrast, the older conventional-drawers ($n = 330$) mainly used regions for the arms (76%) rather than single lines (24%). The pattern was similar for legs: 96% of the tadpole- and transitional-drawers used single lines and only 4% used enclosed regions; among the conventional-drawers, 65% used regions and 35% used single lines.

Segmentation and Contouring

As children add more body parts to their drawings of the human figure, these parts are added on as separate segments (see Fig. 1.7). Each body part may have its own complete boundary and these parts may be placed in very close proximity one to the other in the correct spatial arrangement; alternatively, as each body part is drawn, it may be joined on to the previous part and may share a common boundary. In either case, the figure gives the impression that the child thinks of each body part as a distinct unit.

Instead of building up their figures in this segmented way, a few very young children sketch an outline of the figure as if tracing its silhouette. These contoured figures are generally a later development, however, and according to my data they gradually replace the segmented figures between the ages of 5 and 7 years. Occasionally, children draw the whole outline of the figure in this way, giving it the appearance of a "gingerbread man"; more usually, only certain parts of the figure are subjected to this

FIG. 1.7   Segmented figures drawn by (left) David, aged 5 years 9 months and (right) Laura, aged 5 years 7 months.

FIG. 1.8   Contoured figures drawn by (from left to right) Gary, aged 6 years 5 months, Katherine and Claire, both aged 6 years 11 months.

contouring treatment, the most frequent combination being the torso and the arms or the torso and the legs (Fig. 1.8; see also Chapter 3). Further evidence of this shift from segmentation to contouring comes from a longitudinal study by Fenson (1985) and a cross-sectional study by Eames, Barrett, and McKee (1990).

Volumetric and Surface Representations

Although we may recognise a circle and its facial features as a representation of a head, and an elongated region as a representation of an arm or a leg, the forms themselves are not necessarily used by the child as *surface* representations of these particular body parts seen from the particular viewpoint of an observer. There is evidence (Moore, 1986; Willats, 1985) which indicates that although the shapes on the page capture something of the shape of the real object, young children none the less intend the pictorial form to stand for the *total volume* of the object rather than its surface appearance from one particular vantage point. In Moore's study, for example, when asked to draw a cube placed in front of them, many 7-year-olds drew a single square. Now this square could be interpreted as a surface representation of one face of a cube, but Moore demonstrated that this was not the children's intention: Even though each face of the cube had a different colour, the children did not restrict themselves to only one colour in their drawing; they used many colours, thus indicating that their square stood not for a single face but for the cube as a whole. In contrast, some of the 9-year-olds who had also drawn a single square used only one colour, indicating that they had chosen to depict only one face of the cube.

In a similar way, the circular representation of the head of the young child's tadpole figure may stand for the whole volume of that body part. The inclusion of facial features does not necessarily provide evidence for a surface representation, since these features are likely to be included anyway as defining features of the head. Unambiguous evidence of pictorial forms being used to denote only the surface appearance of body parts rather than the volume of the items as a whole is difficult to find in young children's spontaneous drawings of the human figure. But, one way of gathering such evidence might be to ask the children to draw the back view as well as the front view of a person, as Henderson and Thomas (1990) did in their study of the way that planning for the inclusion of detail might affect the size of the outline (see Chapter 3). These researchers certainly found that all their children, as young as 4 years, did omit the facial features in their back-view drawings; however, all their children were conventional-drawers and we may wish to collect data from tadpole-drawers to see if they, too, are able to depict these different views of the human figure.

Occluding Contours

It appears, then, that young children at least as young as 4 years are capable of adopting different viewpoints of the human figure. These front and back views are not particularly difficult to draw, however; the child needs only to draw the same figure in both cases and to include or omit certain details. If it can be shown that these young children can also draw a figure in, say, full or three-quarters profile, then this would constitute much stronger evidence that they can adopt a different viewpoint *vis-à-vis* the figure. This task is likely to be more difficult, partly because some of the "facts" about the figure have to be sacrificed, e.g. the fact that a person has two eyes and yet, in profile, only one is shown. Another difficulty is that the child may not be able to represent the way that the arm of the profile figure occludes part of the torso.

Young children usually draw their figures facing the viewer and, as far as possible, with each body part occupying its own space (Goodnow, 1977); there is rarely any overlapping. The problem of how one can draw one body part occluding another occurs when children draw figures in profile (see Chapter 3). A line used to indicate the partial occlusion of a background body part by a foreground body part is called an *occluding contour* (Marr, 1977). There is no abrupt change of plane, given that "people are more smooth than they are rectangular" (Willats, 1985, p. 87); the line simply indicates the outer limits of, for example, an arm seen against the torso from a particular point of view. It has been argued that the use of the line as an occluding contour is dependent on the child's ability to adopt a point of view and to see the outline of a figure against its background from a particular angle; for most children, this ability may not occur until at least the age of 7 years (Piaget & Inhelder, 1956). The successful use of occluding contours also involves a certain amount of planning on the part of the drawer: In order to avoid a transparency drawing (in which the contours of unseen body parts are made visible), the body parts nearer to the viewer need to be drawn first and then the more distant parts need to be fitted around these contours (Cox, 1992).

Summary

Although very young children may experiment with making marks on the page for its own sake, they also use the drawing materials in various ways to represent objects and events in the real world. The marks or trails left on the page probably represent the movement or action of an event and are not meant to capture any visual quality of the objects involved. Although children sometimes recognise objects by chance in their scribbles, their early figures seem to be the result of a deliberate intention to draw visually recognisable objects. The problem they are faced with is how to find pictorial forms suitable for denoting the differently shaped parts of an object like the human body. As children add more parts to their figures, they extend their repertoire of denotation forms which discriminate these different body parts. They also show a development away from segmenting each body part towards encompassing larger sections of the figure with a continuous contour and, eventually, to using lines as occluding contours specifying the outer limits of each body part seen against its background from one particular vantage point.

2 The Tadpole Figure

Introduction

The young child's first drawings of the human figure are rather curious in that they seem to consist only of a head, which may include facial features, and legs; if the arms are present, they are attached to the head (see Fig. 2.1). Some other items may be added too, such as hair, ears, hands and feet, but indications that the figure has a tummy or a torso are extremely rare; indeed, the definition of a tadpole form is generally held to be a head–legs figure which has no distinct torso drawn separately from the head (Cox & Parkin, 1986; Cox, 1992). These kinds of figure were noted by Ricci (1887) and have been called cephalopods as well as tadpole figures.

FIG. 2.1 Tadpole figures drawn by children between the ages of 3 years 4 months and 5 years 3 months.

An idea of the body parts included by tadpole-drawers in their drawings of the human figure can be gauged from the data I collected from 133 children. By definition, each tadpole figure had a head and some legs and, again by definition, there was no torso or tummy drawn separately from the head segment, although a mark representing the torso may have been made inside the head contour. The frequencies for other body parts were as follows: eyes 131 (98.5%), mouth 111 (83.5%), nose 78 (58.7%), hair/hat 75 (56.4%), arms 69 (51.9%), feet/shoes 41 (30.8%), hands 19 (14.3%), body/tummy 13 (9.8%), ears 13 (9.8%) and neck 1 (0.8%). The relative popularity or rarity of different body parts is fairly consistent across a number of studies cited in the literature, even though most studies give the breakdown according to the children's ages rather than to the type of figure they have drawn.

Age of Tadpole-drawers

Among my data, the youngest child to have drawn a tadpole figure was aged 2 years 9 months; however, Eng (1931) reported that her niece, Margaret, drew a tadpole at the extraordinarily early age of 1 year 10 months. In the study mentioned above, the ages of the 133 tadpole-drawers ranged from 2 years 11 months to 6 years 2 months with a mean age of 4 years 1 month. These ages are roughly consistent with the findings of a number of studies, many of which have been reviewed by Freeman (1980). Gesell (1925), for example, estimated that between 20 and 49% of 4-year-olds produce a head–legs figure; Ames (1945) expected her "average" children to produce a head–legs figure at the age of 4 years 6 months; Taylor and Bacharach (1981) found that 42% of their 3-year-olds and 45% of their 4-year-olds produced tadpole drawings. By the age of 5 years, most children (67% according to Gesell, 1925) draw a more conventionally structured figure with the torso drawn between the head and the legs and the arms attached to the torso.

Is the Tadpole Figure Copied from Others?

Although nursery school children may have the opportunity to copy tadpole figures from other tadpole-drawers, they also have the opportunity to copy conventional figures drawn by more advanced children or by adults. Young children with older brothers and sisters—as well as only-children—draw tadpoles even when all around them are producing conventional forms and no tadpole drawing is available for them to copy. Most of the human figure drawings that children see in picture- or story-books are conventional figures; so, too, are the figures that adults draw. Although the "Mr Men" series of children's books portrays figures that are very

FIG. 2.2   Children's tadpole figures collected in 1885 and published by Ricci (1887).

similar to tadpole forms, these figures are relatively recent and children were certainly drawing tadpole forms long before these newcomers appeared, as the tadpoles collected by Ricci in 1885 testify (see Fig. 2.2). Thus, the notion that the young child's tadpole form is copied from other sources is very unlikely; it is more likely that it is a discovery or an invention on the part of the child.

Does the Child Lack Knowledge of the Human Form?

Another common argument is that young children's knowledge of the human figure is not sufficiently complete to allow them to draw a conventional figure. Unlikely though it may seem, it has been claimed that young children know only that people are composed of heads and legs. In fact, the evidence indicates clearly that young children are very knowledgeable about the human form and can point to far more features than they include in their drawings.

When 100 tadpole-drawers aged between 2 years 10 months and 4 years 10 months were asked to identify various parts of their bodies, including their "bodies" and "tummies", they could all successfully do so (Cox & Batra, n.d.). Tadpole-drawers can also name body parts; those in a study carried out by Brittain and Chien (1983) could give appropriate names to all of the body parts pointed out by the experimenter on a pre-drawn figure. Thus, tadpole-drawers certainly know that the human figure consists of more than simply a head and some legs, even though they do not display the various parts in their rather minimal tadpole drawings.

Is the Tadpole Figure an Aesthetically "Good Form"?

Kellogg (1969) has argued that the young child's main concern is not with a full and accurate representation of the figure but with a form which is aesthetically well-balanced. In the so-called scribbling stage, according to Kellogg, children build up a repertoire of basic scribbles and then, using these basic scribbles, they create more and more complex forms (see Chapter 1). These forms—for example, *diagrams, combines* and *aggregates* —are guided not by a desire to represent objects but by a sense of aesthetic balance. When children move on to representational drawing, they select a suitable form from this repertoire. The radially symmetrical *mandalas* and *sun-schemas* are particularly well-suited, argues Kellogg, to stand for the human figure; thus the tadpole is not a failed attempt to make a visual likeness to a real person, but a positive adoption of an already well-practised form.

Persuasive though this argument is, the evidence does not support it. As discussed in Chapter 1, rather few of Kellogg's children developed the forms she described and other researchers have been unable to identify the sequential steps that Kellogg advocated. Furthermore, one only has to look at the tadpoles that children first produce in order to see that these forms are rarely radially symmetrical; far more frequently, the legs are elongated and the arms of the figure are omitted altogether.

An Internal Model

From his observation that young children often draw different parts of an object or different parts of a scene in a jumbled fashion, Ricci (1887) suggested that children are not trying to show objects as they see them but, rather, are depicting what they know about them. It is clear though, if we consider the tadpole forms, children do not draw everything they know.

Kerschensteiner (1905) articulated Ricci's notion more clearly and suggested that the child selects only the items which are central to his concept of the object and endeavours to draw these items rather than everything he sees. And Luquet (1913) also argued that, in their attempts to represent an object, children do not draw directly from the object itself but from an internal model or mental image of it, an idea taken up later by Piaget and Inhelder (1969).

Since one cannot reproduce all aspects of a perceived three-dimensional object, we must select certain features from it and re-present them in a more simple and manageable form. For the child, this is likely to be a more difficult task than for the adult and he may select relatively few features. The re-presentation of these features in the form of an internal model or mental image informs or guides the drawing. Thus, the internal model mediates between the child's perception and knowledge of an object on the one hand and his drawing of it on the other. The nature of the internal model, however, has not been specified, although it is often assumed to be some kind of visual image or picture that we inspect inside our heads. Alternatively, it could be a set or list of features that we scan or even a "program" of movements that guides our performance in a certain temporal and spatial order.

The Most Distinguishing Features

A number of researchers (e.g. Elkonin, 1957; Gibson, 1969; Luquet, 1913; Piaget & Inhelder, 1956) agree that the production of a drawing depends on the child having abstracted the distinguishing and invariant features of an object which differentiate it from others; these are then stored as an internal model or, as Gibson (1969, pp. 151–152) calls it, a "memorial representation".

Piaget and Inhelder's (1956) example of young children's drawing of different shapes illustrates how it takes them some time to abstract the necessary features from the object so as to form an adequate internal model. The young child's *perception* of different shapes is not in question; 6-month-old babies can distinguish between a circle and a triangle and, by the age of 2 years, children can correctly distinguish between a square and a diamond (Bee & Walker, 1968; Maccoby & Bee, 1965). They are able to do this not necessarily by exploring each shape systematically but simply by examining it holistically (Zaporozhets, 1965).

The task of drawing one of these shapes, however, is more complex. In this case, the child must analyse each shape in detail; in fact, since objects are normally drawn line by line and section by section in a sequential order, the child must mentally divide the shape into its constituent parts before attempting to reproduce them on the page (Maccoby, 1968). Piaget and Inhelder argued that whereas the younger child's analysis would be somewhat gross (e.g. analysing shapes only as open or closed forms), increasingly they would consider the finer distinctions (e.g. the difference between a circle and an oval or between a square and a diamond). Thus, when children first attempt to draw shapes, they tend to dichotomise them into closed shapes (circle, square, etc.) for which they draw a circular form and open shapes (a cross, horse-shoe, etc.). Next, closed shapes with curves and closed shapes with angles are distinguished but all those in the former group are represented by a circle and those in the latter group by a square. Eventually within these broad categories finer distinctions are made so that, for example, squares, oblongs and triangles are correctly drawn (see Fig. 2.3).

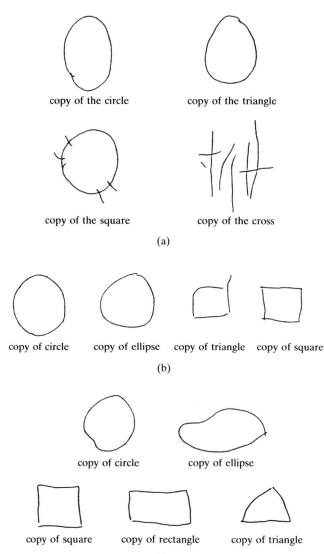

copy of the circle   copy of the triangle

copy of the square   copy of the cross

(a)

copy of circle   copy of ellipse   copy of triangle   copy of square

(b)

copy of circle   copy of ellipse

copy of square   copy of rectangle   copy of triangle

(c)

FIG. 2.3   The development of children's ability to copy geometric figures. (a) At first, the circle is used when copying all closed forms; (b) later, curved and angular shapes are distinguished; and (c) finally, all shapes are distinguished more accurately. (Adapted from Piaget & Inhelder, 1956.)

In a similar way, in the case of the human figure we know that young children can easily recognise both real people and drawings of people. However, we presume that when they begin to draw, young children do not or cannot abstract all of a figure's features but grasp only the most distinguishing ones, namely the head and the legs. And these features constitute the internal model which informs what the child draws. With increasing chronological and mental age, the amount of detail the child abstracts from the object will increase and the drawing itself will become more detailed.

The reason why the head and legs are so important and are abstracted first, so it is claimed, is that the head contains the perceptual apparatus of a person and the legs give the figure its upright stance and also the suggestion of its mobility (Barnes, 1894; Ricci, 1887). It is not clear to me, however, why the arms and the hands are deemed to be less important. Even Golomb, writing in 1988, has endorsed the significance of the head and the legs and talks of the arms as playing a subsidiary role.

Performance Overload

In contrast to this position that the tadpole-drawer's internal model is so minimal, Freeman (1980) has assumed that the tadpole-drawer has a complete internal representation of the human figure which he attempts to draw. Nevertheless, there are still a number of problems which the child encounters and must overcome.

Although he is quite knowledgeable about the human figure and can correctly point to a range of different features, in order to draw the figure the child has to find out which parts are conventionally included and which parts are optional, know how each part might best be drawn, be able to recall all these parts as he is doing the drawing, know where each part goes in relation to the other parts, and be able to fit the parts together on the page. And, of course, he must also have a reasonable amount of control over the fine movements he makes so that the marks go where he intends them to go. The seemingly simple task of drawing a person, then, is in fact a complex and multi-faceted one and it would not be surprising if a child had difficulties with any one of these aspects of the task.

Freeman suggests that it is this performance overload in the drawing task which prevents the child from producing a detailed, conventional figure. In particular, it is the cognitive limitations in the child's accessing of the information contained in the internal model which result in an incomplete drawing. In his account, Freeman (1975; 1980) claims that before drawing the figure, the child scans the internal model from top to bottom (Ghent, 1961; Howard & Templeton, 1966) and holds this information while drawing each segment on the page. We know from the research on serial recall in memory tasks (e.g. Glanzer & Cunitz, 1966) that subjects best remember the first and last items of a list and forget the middle items and so, if primacy and recency effects operate in the drawing task, it is likely that the head and the legs will be included but that the torso will be omitted.

One of the problems with Freeman's explanation is that it is not clear why the head and the legs should be the first and last items on the list. Whereas we can perhaps accept the head as the first item, why are the legs rather than the feet the final item? This problem aside, we can nevertheless test Freeman's explanation by giving tadpole-drawers a task in which most of the production problems of a drawing task have been removed.

A Selection Task

If the tadpole form were to be explained mainly in terms of performance overload and, in particular, as Freeman has suggested, by the child's difficulty in remembering all of the appropriate parts to be drawn, then we could intervene in the drawing process and alleviate the load for the child; he should then produce a more detailed and conventional figure. In fact, two studies have reduced virtually all the performance problems by asking the child not to produce a drawing but to select the picture which "looks most like a real person" (Taylor & Bacharach, 1981) or is "the best picture of a person" (Cox & Stone, cited in Cox, 1992).

In both studies, the children were given a set of pre-drawn forms (see Fig. 2.4): a tadpole, a transitional figure (in which the arms are attached to the legs and a tummy-button was drawn between the legs) and a conventional figure. Surprisingly, perhaps, the tadpole-drawers actually chose a tadpole rather than a conventional figure; indeed, they seemed to have made a deliberate choice in favour of the tadpole form. Furthermore, in our study, not only did 21 out of 25 tadpole-drawers choose the tadpole

FIG. 2.4 The tadpole, transitional and conventional figures presented to children in a selection task. (Reproduced with the permission of Penguin Books Ltd.)

form, but 15 thought that the conventional form was the silliest and 10 thought that the transitional figure was the silliest of the three pictures.

It seems that even when we resolve a large number of the performance problems for the child, as we do in a selection task, tadpole-drawers still fail to select a conventional figure. This throws considerable doubt on Freeman's explanation: tadpole-drawers are not poised to produce a conventional figure if only the production problems were reduced. We are still left with a puzzle, however. We do not know whether the child fails to produce a conventional figure because his internal model is incomplete, or whether the model is complete but inaccessible in some sense, or indeed whether the child simply prefers the tadpole form.

A Shorthand Form

Even though tadpole-drawers have an extensive knowledge of the different body parts of the human figure, they may not necessarily intend to draw a complete figure. Golomb (1981) has argued that they use the tadpole as a kind of shorthand form which readily evokes the idea of a person and is easily recognised as such. As noted earlier, she accepts the claim that the head and legs of the tadpole succinctly encapsulate the human figure for the young child. I assume, then, that Golomb's argument is that although the child selects only a few body parts for his drawing, he nevertheless has a complete internal model of the human figure; Golomb does not explicitly mention the internal model in her account. If this is true, then the child should be able to draw a more conventional figure if he really wanted to or if it was impressed upon him that the conventional figure is the preferred form.

The Dictation Task

We could test Golomb's claim by cueing the tadpole-drawer more forcefully that a conventional form is required and we could do this by naming each body part as the child is about to draw it. In such a task, there are no memory constraints, since the names of the body parts are provided; the child simply has to decide how to draw each part and where it should go in relation to the other parts. If the child is unable to produce a conventional form under these conditions, then this would support Golomb's position (that the child can choose to draw a conventional form if he really wants to). If the child still produces a tadpole, however, then this result would be more in line with the notion that there is some other problem either with the detail of the internal model or with the child's accessing of the information contained within it.

When we dictated the body parts to our six tadpole-drawers (Cox & Parkin, 1986), only one child produced a figure in which the torso was conventionally placed and even in this case the arms were attached to the head. Four children produced their usual tadpole figures and seemed to ignore the instruction to draw a torso; in one figure the arms were omitted, but in the other three they were attached to the "head". Another child simply scribbled when the name of each body part was spoken.

Because we had the impression that the children largely ignored the instructions and simply drew their normal tadpole figure, we repeated the experiment making sure that the children waited and listened for the name of each body part before drawing it. We also had a much larger sample of tadpole-drawers, 25 children with an average age of 3 years 2 months (Cox & Stone, cited in Cox, 1992). This time, only one child ignored the torso; all the others included it in their figures (see Fig. 2.5). Eighteen children placed the torso inside the head contour and only two children placed it below the head as part of a conventional figure. The remaining four children drew the "legs" of the figure when the body was mentioned, and then drew a torso in between the legs when the legs were mentioned. Nearly all of the children placed the arms on the head contour.

FIG. 2.5   The responses of 25 tadpole-drawers in a dictation task.

Most children do not draw a conventional figure even when they are specifically cued to draw the torso after the head and before the legs. They will draw *something* when the torso is named but it is usually a scribble, a dot or a small circle subsumed within another body part, namely the head contour. These findings suggest that tadpole-drawers do not have the option of drawing a conventional figure; there is some particular difficulty which constrains them to producing the tadpole form. From the results of the dictation task, there are at least three possibilities. One is that they have apparently not learned the convention that the torso has its own separate and fairly large contour below that of the head; in fact, judging by the large proportion of children who placed the torso within the head contour, it may even be the case that they normally incorporate the torso within it. Secondly, it may be that the torso is in fact missing, the reason being that the children have not devised a way of drawing it. And, thirdly, there is still the possibility that the child's internal model is incomplete and that this minimal form is replicated in the child's graphic production.

The Undifferentiated Tadpole

The suggestion mentioned above that the torso is in fact already included in the tadpole form was advocated by Arnheim (1974). According to him, the child's internal model of the human form is complete but the head and the torso are undifferentiated. When the child comes to draw the figure, he retains this "fused" form and produces a tadpole in which the head contour is actually a head–torso conglomerate. Viewed in this way, the tadpole figure seems less bizarre and the positioning of the arms, if they are included, suggests that the child may have attached them to the torso rather than to the head.

One way to find out if the torso has been included in the figure is simply to ask the child what each part of his tadpole is meant to represent. However, of the 100 tadpole-drawers reported earlier (Cox & Batra, n.d.), only one child had drawn a tummy-button on his tadpole-figure and none of the other 99 mentioned a tummy-button, a torso or a body when asked to identify each part of the tadpole indicated by the experimenter. In a further study of 133 tadpole-drawers (reported earlier in this chapter), only 13 (9.8%) had drawn, or had said that their figure included, a torso. If the head contour really does include a torso, it is odd that so very few children mentioned it.

It might be objected, however, that this kind of questioning was too gross in the sense that the experimenter pointed to the whole head contour and then to the legs. It could be that even if the child said "head" when the experimenter indicated the whole head contour, this contour might still have had a torso subsumed within it. One of my students, Helen Windybank, introduced a more detailed identification task. When the child had drawn his tadpole figure, the experimenter pointed to various specific locations with her pencil point. These included six points: the upper and lower parts of the circle, the upper and lower parts of a leg, the upper and lower parts of the leg-space (see Fig. 2.6).

Windybank tested 65 tadpole-drawers aged between 3 years 3 months and 5 years (mean age 3 years 10 months). Nine of these children were unable to grasp the instructions of the task and either declined to point or pointed to the same body part for all six items; these children were omitted from the analysis. For locations A and B, most children (93 and 77%, respectively) pointed to their heads (see Fig. 2.6). For locations E and F, most children pointed to their legs (84 and 86%, respectively). The modal response for locations C (52%) and D (63%) was the legs. Overall, only a minority of children pointed to their torsos.

FIG. 2.6 As the experimenter pointed to each of six points on their tadpole figure, the children themselves were asked to point to the same place on their own bodies.

This evidence suggests that, on the whole, the tadpole is a tadpole—that is, a head and legs—and that there is no hidden or undifferentiated torso incorporated in it. Why, then, did most of the children in the dictation task locate the body *inside* the head contour? It may be that they were expecting the legs to be named after items relating to the head, but when the body was named instead they may have assumed that such an unusual item (i.e. not normally part of their schema) must be related to the part already drawn, namely the head.

Where Should the Torso Go?

Although most children seem not to have included a torso in their tadpole figure, if they are asked where the tummy or the body is or should be they will indicate its location (Cox, 1989; 1992; Cox & Batra, n.d.; Cox & Jarvis, n.d.). For example, in Cox and Batra's study, when asked where the tummy was located, 93 out of 100 children either drew a mark or pointed to a place on their figure; 7 children said that their figure didn't have a tummy, or that they couldn't draw one, or that they didn't know where it was.

This readiness to respond, however, cannot be accepted as evidence for Arnheim's (1974) claim that the torso has already been included in the tadpole; rather, it may simply indicate that the children interpret the experimenter's question as implying that the torso is missing and that they should indicate where it should go, and indeed many children respond to the question by immediately adding a little mark for the torso.

If tadpole-drawers know that the torso is in fact located below the head and above the legs, then we might expect them to indicate a location on their tadpole figures where the head and legs meet. Most normal children at this age are quite capable of specifying such a precise location. In fact, among the large number of tadpole-drawers in the studies by Cox and Batra and Cox and Jarvis, no child did this. Of the 93 children who indicated the tummy on their figure when questioned by Cox and Batra, 46 located it within the head of the tadpole and 47 located it in the space between the legs. Of the 72 children questioned by Cox and Jarvis, 34 children indicated a place within the head and 38 indicated a place between the legs.

Since roughly half the children in both these studies located the tummy within the head segment and half located it between the legs, we might reasonably regard the location of the tummy as a matter of chance. Goodnow (1977), however, has claimed that the responses are associated with the relative proportions of the tadpole figure, so that the tummy is located in the head if that segment is longer and between the legs if those are longer. The studies by Cox and Batra and Cox and Jarvis have supported Goodnow's claim. Cox and Jarvis also found that the location of the tummy and the relative lengths of the head and legs segments correlated with the position of the facial features: if the head is longer, the facial features tend to be placed in its upper portion and the tummy in its lower part; if the legs are longer, the facial features tend to be centrally placed in the head and the tummy is located between the legs.

What may be happening in these correlational studies is that the children may be reacting to the completed figure, saying that the torso is contained in whichever body part happens to be longer. If this were so, then they should change their location of the torso depending on the proportions of the figure. Cox and Jarvis (n.d.) gave tadpole-drawers aged 3 years 5 months to 4 years 3 months, some pre-drawn tadpoles in which the relative lengths of the head and legs had been varied; that is, the head was longer than the legs in one drawing, and the legs were relatively longer than the head in the other. The result was that the children continued to locate the torso in the same body section as in their own drawing. So, for example, a child who had drawn the torso in the head contour went on doing so even when the head was quite small and the facial features filled it up. In order to check for immediate carry-over effects, we compared a group of children who completed the pre-drawn figures immediately after their first drawing with another group who had a day's gap in between. In fact, most of the children in both groups continued to locate the torso in the same place.

Clearly, tadpole-drawers do not readily switch the location of the torso when they are presented with a differently proportioned figure. This may not mean, however, that the proportions of their first figure did not influence their choice of location for the torso. It may be that the children did locate the torso according to the proportions of the first figure (which may in itself have been their usual, well-practised figure) and then they repeated that location in later figures.

The Manikin Task

Since children can correctly point to their own body parts, including the torso, and can also name the body parts on a human figure drawing, we can assume that they know that the torso is located below the head and above the legs. However, when asked where the torso should go on their tadpole figures, they do not indicate this precise location where the head and legs meet; rather, they indicate a location either within the head contour or between the legs. It may be that tadpole-drawers do not, or cannot, "re-think" their tadpole figure and consider how it could be reorganised to incorporate a complete new segment. In fact, Karmiloff-Smith (1986; 1990) has argued for just such an explanation for a young child's apparent inability to modify her figures. Although this position has been articulated in relation to slightly older children and will be set out more fully in Chapter 3, the essential argument is that young children cannot modify an already practised procedure if that modification is required mid-procedure. The addition of a torso to a child's tadpole figure would certainly constitute such a modification, since, essentially, the two main elements of the tadpole, the head and the legs, have to be separated so that the torso can be inserted between them. Another reason mentioned earlier for children's failure to produce conventional figures when the parts were dictated to them is that they do not know *how* to draw the torso; although most of the children in the dictation task drew *something* when the torso was mentioned, they tended to draw a squiggle or a small circle.

One way that we could check these possibilities would be to provide all the key parts of a conventional form, including the torso, and to ask the child to construct a manikin. Since the body parts would be provided, the child would not need to devise a way of representing them but would simply need to assemble them in a conventional spatial arrangement. If the child already knows where the torso should be located on a conventional figure, then he should be able to assemble the manikin correctly. If he cannot do this, then the problem must be one of inadequate knowledge about the spatial layout of the figure. When we asked six tadpole-drawers to construct a person out of a number of ready-cut pieces of card (Cox & Parkin, 1986), only one child constructed a conventional figure. Bassett (1977), in contrast, obtained much better results: all 12 of her tadpole-drawers produced conventional forms, apparently placing the arms on the torso.

There were at least two important differences between these two studies which may have accounted for the contrasting results. First, the shapes of the manikin pieces were different (see Fig. 2.7); whereas we used a smaller and a larger circle, Bassett used a round shape and an oblong shape. It is possible that in our study the children did not recognise so readily that one of the circles was meant to represent a torso; some children simply ignored the second circle, whereas others made two tadpoles from the two circles and two sets of limbs. The circle and rectangle in Bassett's study were perhaps more easily distinguished as being likely representations of the head and the torso, respectively. The second difference between the two studies was that Bassett's tadpole-drawers were much older than ours; the mean age of her children was 4 years 9 months, whereas the mean age of our children was 3 years 1 month. It could be that Bassett's children were much closer to relinquishing their tadpole figures and moving towards conventional forms.

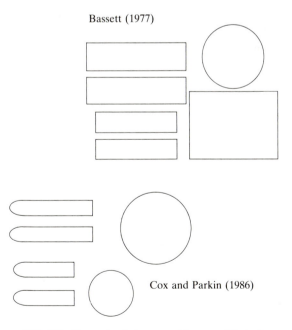

Bassett (1977)

Cox and Parkin (1986)

FIG. 2.7   Two sets of pieces used in a manikin task.

Stephanie Osmond and I compared the manikins produced by 13 tadpole-drawers (mean age 3 years 8 months) who used Bassett's pieces and 13 (mean age 3 years 10 months) who used Cox and Parkin's pieces. Eleven out of 13 children produced conventional figures using Bassett's pieces, whereas 7 out of 13 did so using Cox and Parkin's pieces. Another student, Helen Windybank, has also replicated these findings with tadpole-drawers with a mean age of 3 years 10 months: 20 out of 32 children produced conventional figures with Bassett's pieces, whereas only 8 out of 33 children produced them with Cox and Parkin's pieces.

Bassett's pieces are probably more successful because children easily recognise that the circular piece is meant to be a head and that the rectangular piece is meant to be a torso. The second circle among Cox and Parkin's pieces probably does not convey the notion of a torso and, since they may not be searching for one, the children simply ignore it or construct two tadpoles with the two circles and two sets of limbs.

Although most of those children who used Bassett's pieces constructed a conventional form, a few did not. It may be that for these children the rectangle was not acceptable as a torso or was simply not recognised as representing one. If the rectangle had been more clearly identifiable as a torso, then perhaps all the children would have used it. Indeed, there is some evidence from studies by Gesell (1925), Ames (1943; 1945), Ames and Ilg (1963) and Golomb (1973) that all tadpole-drawers are able to complete a manikin task when the body parts have identifying features on them.

Ruth Stoker and I gave Bassett's pieces to 11 tadpole-drawers and the same pieces with features drawn on them to a second group of 10 tadpole-drawers (see Fig. 2.8). The mean age of both groups was 4 years 4 months. Nine of the 11 children using the blank pieces produced conventional figures, but all 10 of those using the featured pieces were successful. The 11 children who had the blank pieces first were then given the featured pieces after a delay of at least 30 min; all of them constructed a conventional form. Similarly, those who had used the featured pieces first were then given the blank pieces; all of them produced a conventional form except one who constructed a transitional figure, placing the arms on the legs and omitting the torso altogether.

Clearly, when tadpole-drawers are given a recognisable representation of the torso along with the other main body parts, they are able to construct a conventional figure. They know where to place the torso in relation to the head and the legs and, furthermore, they place the arms on the torso and not on the head or the legs. Although the manikin task is a construction task and not a drawing task, the fact that tadpole-drawers can construct a conventional figure shows that they can modify their pictorial representation of a person and, furthermore, that they can make

FIG. 2.8   Blank and featured pieces used in a manikin task.

modifications during their normal procedure and not only at the end of it as Karmiloff-Smith (1986; 1990) has advocated (see Chapter 3).

The Position of the Arms

Whereas the omission or the inclusion of the torso in the tadpole figure is not always absolutely clear, the inclusion or omission of the arms is usually obvious. Furthermore, when they are present, the representation of the arms is usually conventional in the sense that they are drawn as single lines protruding more or less horizontally from the sides of the figure; children who have begun to draw conventional figures draw the arms in a similar way.

Even in a conventional figure, the arms are usually the last item to be drawn, after the head contour, facial features, torso and legs. They are also frequently the last item to be included in the tadpole. And this is reckoned to be precisely why they may be left out—they have simply been forgotten. Among conventional-drawers themselves, many even at 5 years of age omit the arms (Gesell, 1925; Hurlock & Thomson, 1934; Partridge, 1902).

The issue regarding the arms is not whether they have been included or omitted, but whether they have been correctly positioned, and this, in turn, is related to our interpretation of the "head" of the tadpole. The placement of the arms on the head contour should not surprise us if we believe that the head contour also encompasses the torso; but, since the evidence does not in fact support this "conglomerate" interpretation of the head contour, the positioning of the arms on the head is rather bizarre and requires explanation.

Freeman (1975) investigated tadpole-drawers' intentions about the positioning of the arms by asking them to draw the missing arms onto some pre-drawn conventional figures; these pre-drawn figures varied in their head/torso proportions. He found that the tadpole-drawers (and also some scribblers) could draw the arms onto the figure, thus supporting the notion that, at least for arms, their internal model is complete, that they have devised a means of representing arms and that when cued they will include them. A curious finding, however, was that the location of the arms shifted depending on which part was the larger, the head or the torso. Freeman called this *the body-proportion effect*, an effect which persisted even when the children's attention was directed to the torso by asking them to draw in the tummy-button first (Freeman & Hargreaves, 1977). On the basis of these findings, Freeman has argued that the placement of the arms is not fixed, but is affected by the arrangement or proportion of the figure already drawn. And, in the case of the tadpole figure in which there is only one enclosed unit (the head), the arms are attached to it.

Taking Stock

From the evidence presented above, it seems that tadpole-drawers are extremely reluctant to relinquish their tadpole form. They eschew the opportunity to select a conventional form even when a ready-drawn example is available and most of them fail to construct a conventional figure when the body parts are dictated to them. In the dictation task, they will make a mark for the torso when it is named, but they have little idea about how it should or could be represented. These findings suggest that it is unlikely that there is a conventional form "waiting to come out", if only we could remove some of the performance difficulties in the task, as Freeman has suggested, or simply cue the child that the conventional form is the appropriate form to choose (which would accord with Golomb's explanation).

The most likely explanation for the omission of the torso appears to be that the child has not devised a suitable graphic schema for it, perhaps because the torso is deemed to be less important than the head and legs. When a recognisable torso is supplied, the tadpole-drawer will construct a conventional figure.

The arms are often omitted apparently because the child has forgotten them; if reminded (in a dictation task, for example), then tadpole-drawers will include them, and if a suitable representation of the torso is provided (in a manikin task), the arms will be attached to it.

Teaching the Conventional Form

Although all normal children eventually draw a conventional form, I was keen to find out whether they could be taught how to draw it. On the one hand, the tadpole form seems to be so entrenched that it may be difficult to supplant; on the other, there is evidence that some children, at least, learn the conventional form by direct teaching (see, for example, the cases cited by Cox and Parkin, 1986). Since these children most probably learned the conventional figure by observing and copying the conventional form being drawn, I chose a copying task as the most appropriate teaching medium. If the child is asked to copy an adult's drawing of a person, he is relieved of a number of problems: he is told which items to include and when to include them, he is shown how to draw each item, he is shown where each item is located and he is shown how it fixes on.

I gave this task to a number of tadpole-drawers who were allocated to different experimental groups (Cox, 1992). In the *whole figure* group, 22 tadpole-drawers watched the human figure being drawn and listened to each part being named. Twelve of the children (55%) drew a conventional form when they were asked to copy this model. Another group of 22 children copied each segment of the figure as the experimenter drew it— this was the *segment* group. Fifteen of these children (68%) drew a conventional form. Yet another group of children ($n = 18$) copied three of these segment-by-segment figures—this was the *repeated segment* group. By the third figure, 13 of the 18 children (72%) drew conventional forms. A control group of 22 tadpole-drawers all drew tadpoles. A further control group ($n = 14$) was asked to draw three more figures, but these were all tadpoles, thus confirming that simply repeating the drawing task without tuition would not lead to a conventional figure being produced.

All of the children were asked to draw a figure again 2 days later. All of the control children drew tadpoles. In the whole figure group, seven of the conventional drawers reverted to drawing tadpoles, which reduced the number who drew conventional figures to five (23%). The same thing happened in the segment group. It was only in the repeated segment group that the majority of the figures were conventional forms on the second visit: 10 of the 13 conventional-drawers continued with their conventional form, one tadpole-drawer changed to the conventional form, and 3 conventional drawers reverted to the tadpole form—leaving 11 out of 18 conventional-drawers.

This copying task indicates that in order to draw a conventional form, children need to be told not only to include the torso but also to see how it is drawn and how it is fitted into the total figure. Even then it is only when they are given the opportunity to copy each item step-by-step and are able to practise the task over a number of trials that they are successful.

Longitudinal Data

Tadpole figures are so common among young children's human figure drawings that, as Freeman (1980, p. 284) notes, they are probably drawn by all children, in Western societies at least. However, since most studies have been cross-sectional in design, it is difficult to assess how long the tadpole phase lasts for each individual child and whether a proportion of children develop their human figure drawings without going through a tadpole phase at all.

There are a few longitudinal single case studies in the literature (e.g. Eng, 1931; Luquet, 1913), all of which indicate that children do go through a tadpole phase before moving on to drawing the human figure in a conventional form. Cox and Parkin (1986) also carried out a longitudinal study of six children over a 1-year period; the children were between the ages of 2 years 7 months and 2 years 9 months at the beginning of the study and were all scribblers. As well as asking the children to make a human figure drawing at 2-monthly intervals, we also collected the children's spontaneous drawings in order to obtain as complete a record as possible of their drawing development. Four of the six children produced tadpole figures before moving on to the conventional form, but as far as we know the other two did not. There was evidence, however, that these two children were atypical in the sense that they may have been shown how to draw a conventional figure: One child, Joe, explicitly said that his friend had shown him how to draw giants and the other child, Simon, had drawn a stick figure which is unusual in very young children's drawings (see Chapter 3) and which may have been introduced to him by an adult.

The children in Cox and Parkin's study had very different patterns of progress regarding their drawings of the human figure. Some children exhibited a short but distinct tadpole phase which was clearly superseded by the introduction of the conventional form; others exhibited a longer period of 6–10 months in which, although the tadpole form emerged first, both the tadpole and conventional forms were drawn before the conventional form became dominant in the end. Since the two forms may co-exist in this way, it is clearly not the case that all children move abruptly from one stage to another; it seems more likely that even when some children have developed a new form, they may still find uses for the old form too. It may be that these children use the conventional form when the human figure is the main topic of the picture but revert to the tadpole form as a "shorthand" when a single human figure is less dominant in the scene, when for instance the child draws a scene involving some group activity (Cox, 1992).

The Transitional Form

Two forms of the tadpole figure were noted by Luquet (1920), Gridley (1938) and Arnheim (1974). In one form, the head is usually longer and items conventionally attached to the torso are attached to the head of the figure; in the other form, the legs are usually longer, the torso is located between the legs and the arms are also attached to them (see Fig. 2.9). This second form of tadpole has been termed *transitional* by Cox and Parkin (1986), who noted that it was drawn by children older than those who drew the standard tadpole. Although the exact mean ages differ from study to study, this age difference between tadpole and transitional drawers appears to be a consistent finding.

FIG. 2.9   Transitional figures drawn by children aged 4 years 2 months and 4 years 9 months.

As well as this evidence from cross-sectional studies, there is additional evidence from a longitudinal study (Cox & Parkin, 1986). Although not all of the children in this study drew transitional forms, those who did did so after they had drawn the standard tadpole. Further evidence that the transitional figure is a more "mature" form comes from Cox and Stone's study (cited in Cox, 1992) in which children were asked to select the best figure from a set of three—a tadpole, a transitional figure and a conventional figure. Twenty-one of the 25 tadpole-drawers chose the pre-drawn tadpole form; in contrast, 22 of 30 transitional-drawers chose the conventional figure and all of the conventional-drawers chose this figure. Thus, tadpole-drawers seem to be entrenched in their own style, as Taylor and Bacharach (1981) also found, whereas transitional-drawers appear to aspire towards the conventional form even though they fall short of producing it themselves.

It has been argued by Goodnow (1977), for example, that the conventional figure develops out of the tadpole or transitional form. Simply by placing a cross-line between the legs of the figure, the child can construct a fully enclosed torso segment and the arms, if they are included, can then be attached to the sides. This description of the development is attractive because it suggests that the young child develops by adapting an already practised form in a relatively minimal way. If this were true, however, we would expect to see large numbers of rectangular torsos in children's early conventional figures; in fact, although some children probably do develop their figures in this way, most children add a new, circular or oval torso to their figures and then attach the legs to this segment.

A Mixture of Styles

The rigidly schematic drawings typical of young children (a characteristic referred to as *type constancy*) were taken by Luquet (1913; 1927) as evidence for the existence of a stable internal model which contains enduring information about the object rather than the changing and often atypical "snapshot" views of it as seen from different angles. Now, as Luquet observed, many children do draw their figures in the same way over a period of time, including the same number of body parts and fixing them together in the same way, and as we have seen in the studies I have cited in this chapter, many children seem extremely reluctant to change their style even when given heavily cued tasks.

Some children, in contrast, fluctuate considerably and draw their figures with varying amounts of detail, sometimes adding arms, for example, and sometimes omitting them; a few children, like Eng's niece Margaret (Eng, 1931), make more dramatic changes, drawing tadpoles, transitional figures and conventional figures even on the same piece of paper (see Fig. 2.10).

FIG. 2.10   A bear, a monkey and a person drawn by Margaret, aged 4 years 5 months. (From Eng, 1931.)

If we assume, as the evidence suggests, that the child's internal model is complete, then we must consider why some children are sometimes able to replicate the model on the page but at other times do not do so. It may be that the explanations put forward by Freeman and by Golomb are relevant in these cases. According to Freeman, because of memory limitations, the child fails to access some of the items in his otherwise complete internal model. Although the evidence does not support this position as the main explanation for the tadpole form, it may nevertheless explain why some children draw fewer details on some occasions than on others; it may be that lapses in attention result in certain items being omitted.

The other explanation is based on Golomb's view that, although children have a complete knowledge of the figure, they choose to draw a less complete form: When some children intermix their styles, they may simply choose different forms on different occasions; thus, the child may simply alter his intentions from one drawing to another. In fact, his intentions may be influenced by the context of the task; for example, a child is perhaps more likely to use a minimal form when he is simply adding incidental figures to a larger scene, but a more detailed form when the human figure itself is the primary topic of the picture (Cox, 1992).

Summary

The child's early attempts to draw the human figure are called *tadpoles*. They seem to consist only of a head and two legs, and the arms—if included at all—appear to be attached to the head of the figure. These tadpole forms are drawn by most children around the ages of 3–4 years.

It is clear that tadpole-drawers have a much more complete and detailed knowledge of the human body than the tadpole form itself implies, so that the tadpole cannot be a simple reflection of the child's incomplete or defective knowledge. Indeed, it has been suggested that children do not draw directly from a real object at all but from their internal model of a real object. It may be that their internal model is undifferentiated and that the tadpole drawing itself really contains an undifferentiated head–torso conglomerate. There is, however, little evidence to support this claim as tadpole-drawers very rarely indicate that their figure has a torso.

An alternative explanation is that the internal model is incomplete. It is by no means straightforward, however, to make this assumption, because there are also performance problems which might interfere with a child's transfer of his internal model to the graphic output on the page. Thus, the child's internal model might be complete but he might be unable to access all of it. And, further, we must consider what the child's intention actually is. Even if a child's knowledge of the human figure is complete and detailed, even if his internal model is complete and detailed and even if he is not burdened by production problems, he may none the less decide to represent the human figure in a "shorthand" form and may not choose to present it in the most detailed way he can.

In order to disentangle these different explanations, a number of studies have manipulated the performance demands of the task. Even when it has been made clear to the child that a complete figure is required rather than a shorthand form, and when various performance problems, including those relating to memory, have been excluded from the task, children still persist in drawing tadpole forms. Not only do they appear to prefer this form, but they also seem to be unable to draw a conventional figure. It is only after a number of attempts at copying an adult's conventional figure in a step-by-step way that tadpole-drawers seem able to draw a conventional form.

It is tempting to accept the explanation that the tadpole-drawers' internal model of the human figure is incomplete. However, the evidence from the manikin tasks suggests that we might be wrong in coming to this conclusion. When tadpole-drawers are provided with a recognisable representation of a torso and are simply required to assemble a figure, they readily include the torso in their construction and they produce a conventional figure. Thus, the reason for the omission of the torso in their tadpole drawings appears to be that children have not yet devised a way of representing it. And this delay may reflect the lesser importance of the torso in the basic representation of the human figure. The reason for the omission of the arms in many tadpole figures is that they have simply been forgotten. When reminded, tadpole-drawers will add the arms, although they will usually be misplaced since the torso itself is missing; when the torso is present, in a manikin construction, the children will locate the arms correctly.

The evidence suggests that tadpole-drawers have considerable knowledge of the human figure and that their internal model is complete (I shall discuss this further in Chapter 8). When they first begin to draw, however, they may have priorities regarding the importance of particular body parts and may not have worked out ways of representing the less important parts. Furthermore, they may also forget to include some parts for which they have in fact worked out an adequate representation. Yet another factor which may lead to the persistence of the tadpole form is that it becomes well-practised so that the child may produce it almost "automatically" without considering how it might be adapted to accommodate new parts; despite this seemingly automatic procedure, however, tadpole-drawers are capable to some extent of reorganising their schemas. A final reason for retaining the tadpole form may be that it is easily recognised as a human form and therefore the child may feel no pressing need to alter it.

With increasing chronological and mental age, the child adds more body parts to the figure and by the age of 5 or 6 years these are put together in a conventional form. We presume that in order to do this the child becomes increasingly concerned with the realism of the figure and devises ways of representing more and more body parts. For some children, there seem to be distinct stages between their different styles of drawing the human figure, but with others the occurrence of tadpoles, transitional figures and conventional figures overlap and co-exist over a period of time before the conventional form eventually dominates.

Although this general shift is related to chronological and mental age (Barnard & Freeman, 1983; Cox & Howarth, 1989; Golomb & Barr-Grossman, 1977), tadpole and transitional figures are also found in some normal adults who have had little or no experience of drawing (e.g. Alland, 1983; Cox & Bayraktar, 1989). These cases suggest that it may be more useful to think of the tadpole form not as a developmentally immature way of representing the human figure, but as an early prototype tried out by people who are basically novices at the drawing task. It is not necessarily the case, however, that all novice drawers, child or adult, will necessarily produce the tadpole form. As we shall see in Chapter 7, there are many societies in which quite different forms of the human figure are produced and this implies that those aspects of the human figure chosen as distinguishing features by Western drawers are not necessarily universal.

3 Children's Modifications of Their Human Figure Drawings

The Introduction of the Torso

The inclusion of the torso below the head is a particularly important "milestone" and occurs in most children's drawings by the age of about 5–6 years. This addition has the effect of making the figure more "normal", if still childlike, in appearance. In fact, the presence of the torso is probably the main criterion of what is known as a *conventional* human figure drawing (Cox & Parkin, 1986). When I collected 454 figure drawings (Cox, unpublished data) from children between the ages of 2 years and 7 years 6 months, I found that 404 were recognisable human forms; the majority were conventional figures, although some were tadpoles and transitional figures (see Chapter 2). The mean age of the 60 tadpole-drawers was 3 years 11 months, the 14 transitional-drawers 4 years and the 330 conventional drawers 5 years 6 months.

Adding More Body Parts

Up to the age of about 12 or 13 years, children add more and more body parts to their drawings of the human figure (Goodenough, 1926; Harris, 1963; Koppitz, 1968; Partridge, 1902); after that age they become more interested in drawing portraits rather than whole figures and, in addition, pay more attention to the modelling or shading of the head than to the inclusion of more details. The frequencies of inclusion of various body parts by the children in my study are shown in Table 3.1 (percentages are given in parentheses). Some parts, such as the head and the legs, are by

TABLE 3.1

Frequencies of Body Parts Drawn by Tadpole- and Transitional-drawers and by Conventional-drawers (Percentages in Parentheses)

	Tadpole- and Transitional-drawers[a] (n = 74)	Conventional-drawers[b] (n = 330)
Head	74 (100)	330 (100)
Body/tummy	4 (5)	330 (100)
Legs	74 (100)	326 (99)
Arms	45 (61)	294 (89)
Eyes	73 (99)	326 (99)
Nose	42 (57)	261 (79)
Mouth	56 (76)	309 (94)
Hair/hat	33 (45)	264 (80)
Ears	8 (11)	44 (13)
Hands	15 (20)	227 (69)
Feet/shoes	26 (35)	257 (78)
Neck	1 (1)	51 (15)

[a] Mean age 4 years; [b] mean age 5 years 6 months.

TABLE 3.2

Percentages of Body Parts Drawn by Children Aged 6–15 Years in 1939

	Age (Years)									
	6	7	8	9	10	11	12	13	14	15
View of figure and face										
Front	71	58	46	35	25	24	25	34	42	56
Back	–	–	1	1	2	3	1	–	–	–
Mixed profile	1	1	1	3	6	4	2	2	3	5
Profile	25	39	51	60	66	68	69	63	54	38
Three-quarters turn	3	2	1	1	1	1	1	1	1	1
Head										
Hair	25	32	40	52	65	68	70	70	58	45
Eyebrows	10	12	15	18	22	25	30	33	35	30
Eye details	–	–	–	–	–	1	1	1	1	1
Ears	5	7	10	15	22	28	34	40	45	48
Nose detail	18	20	25	25	25	24	20	20	18	8
Chin	2	6	12	22	32	36	40	44	46	50
Figure										
Neck	42	45	49	55	68	75	77	80	84	90
Shoulders	2	2	4	8	12	18	22	28	35	40
Waist	2	2	3	10	15	20	22	24	24	12
Chest	1	1	2	4	6	9	12	16	18	6
Hands	40	50	60	66	70	72	74	72	70	50
Fingers	15	15	15	15	16	18	20	22	25	28
Exactly five fingers	5	5	5	5	5	6	7	8	8	8
Shoes or toes	2	2	3	10	15	20	22	24	24	12

definition included in the tadpole and transitional forms; other parts, such as the eyes and the mouth, are also very frequently found in the tadpole figure. Most other body parts are much less frequent at this early stage but are relatively common in the conventional figure. Body parts which still remain less common throughout are the ears and the neck.

In 1939, Lark-Horovitz carried out a study of children's drawing in Cleveland, Ohio, in which 864 children between the ages of 6 and 15 years participated (data reported in Lark-Horovitz, Lewis, & Luca, 1973). The frequencies for the inclusion of various body parts in a "Draw a picture of a man" task are shown in Table 3.2. Ears are as uncommon among the younger children's drawings in the Cleveland data as they are among mine. There are, however, some anomalies: hair and shoes/toes appear relatively less frequently and necks much more frequently among the Cleveland 6-year-olds' drawings than they do among mine. In order to check the reliability of my findings, I collected another sample of drawings, this time from 446 children between the ages of 2 years 3 months and 7 years 4 months. The pattern of frequencies was very similar to that in my first sample and, in particular, the inclusion of ears and the neck was again very rare (13 and 11% of the conventional drawers, respectively), whereas the inclusion of feet/shoes was quite common (66%).

The Head and the Torso

Each of the body parts of children's early figure drawings tends to have its own *line* or *region*, and Willats (1985; 1987; see also Chapter 1) gives an explanation of the child's choice of line or region depending on the salient dimensions of the particular body part of a real person. Since the head and torso are fairly bulky objects, children are likely to depict them with regions. Some children draw the torso with its own complete contour, touching the head at the "neck"; others draw an elongated arc for the torso and link its two ends onto the base of the head contour so that the two body parts have a shared boundary (see Fig. 1.7). Among a group of 150 children who had drawn a curvilinear segment for the torso of their figure, I found that 48 drew it as a completely separate segment, whereas 102 attached it to the head contour. There was a slight but non-significant age difference between these groups—the children drawing a separate segment had a mean age of 5 years 2 months and those linking the torso segment to the head had a mean age of 5 years 5 months. Very few children draw a single line for the torso (Kellogg, 1969, p. 108), even though adults sometimes use this form when drawing figures for young children. In fact, in my sample of 330 conventional-drawers, only one child drew a line for the torso. With increasing age, children continue to use enclosed regions for the head and the torso of their figures, and they become more proficient at altering the shapes of those body parts.

Arms and Legs

In contrast to the bulky head and torso, arms and legs are long objects which young children are likely to depict with single lines (Willats, 1985; 1987). This was borne out by my data: 84% of the tadpole- and transitional-drawers who added arms to their figures used single lines and 96% used single lines for legs. However, with increasing age, children do not continue to use single lines for the limbs: Among my conventional-drawers, 76% drew double lines for the arms and 65% drew double lines for the legs (see Fig. 1.8). Thus, children change from using single lines to using elongated regions. These findings support those in other research studies that by the age of about 6 years, most children draw double lines to represent the limbs (Koppitz, 1968; Papadakis-Michaelides, 1989). Interestingly, however, my data do not support Partridge's (1902) claim that double lines are used for legs earlier than they are for arms. The shift from using single lines to elongated regions for the limbs may be related to an increasing desire for greater visual realism (Fenson, 1985); although the limbs do saliently extend in one particular dimension (Willats, 1985; 1987), they also present an elongated area to the visual field (see Chapter 1).

From Segmentation to Contouring

As each feature is added, it is clearly delineated so that the overall figure has a segmented appearance. Increasingly, however, children begin to use a continuous contour (called *threading* by Goodnow, 1977) to combine previously segmented body parts; so, for example, the arms and the upper torso or the lower torso and the legs may be "run together" to form one unit (see Fig. 1.8). This age-related change has also been noted by Fenson (1985) in a single-case, longitudinal study, by Reith (1988) in a "drawing from life" task, and by Eames et al. (1990) in a two-dimensional copying task. In a sample of 118 "draw a person" figures produced by children between the ages of 5 and 6 years, I found that 74% were segmented and only 26% showed any indication of contouring. Among a sample of 127 seven- to eight-year-olds, however, 81% were using some form of con-touring and among 99 nine- to ten-year-olds 96% were doing so.

Two reasons why children may change their style of depiction from a segmented to a contouring style have been suggested by Fenson (1985). One is that children strive for realism and this necessitates the abandon-ment of a segmented style because rigidly, segmented parts of a figure are not readily apparent in real figures or in realistic paintings of them. The second reason is that children become more interested in depicting the figure engaged in some activity and this emphasis leads them to discover more flexible modes of representation.

Whereas it is difficult to test the first of these explanations, the second can be checked more easily. I compared the set of standard figure drawings mentioned above with those drawn by a second sample of children in the same three age groups, who were asked to draw a person running. It turned out, in fact, that those children in the "running" condition did not produce more contoured figures than those who drew a standard figure (see Table 3.3). The 5- to 6-year-olds drew mainly segmented figures in both conditions, whereas the children in the two older groups drew contoured figures. So, at least the second of Fenson's suggestions for an increase in contouring can be discounted.

When I examined the actual body segments that the children combined in their contoured figures, I found that the most frequent combination was the upper torso and the arms or the lower torso and the legs, which often gave the figure the appearance of being clothed in a jumper or jacket or some trousers; 59% of 5- to 6-year-olds and 68% of 7- to 8-year-olds displayed this kind of contouring. A second, less frequent combination of body parts was the leg and foot or arm and hand; 45% of 5- to 6-year-olds and 58% of 7- to 8-year-olds displayed this kind of contouring. Most children were in fact either "clothes contourers" or "limb contourers", and only a minority of children used both kinds of contouring. Incidentally, the increasing use of contouring for clothing a figure may account for the increase in the inclusion of the arms; the arms are automatically included in the new schema for the jumper or jacket unit and are therefore unlikely to be forgotten. A much smaller category of contouring combined the neck and the upper torso, and this accounted for just one case at age 5–6 years, rising to 19% at age 7–8 years.

These findings suggest that children may have two main interests in contouring their figures: the first—accounting for the majority—is in the

TABLE 3.3
Frequency of Segmented or Contoured Figures Drawn by Children of Three Age Levels in Two Conditions

	Standard		Running	
Age Group	Segmented	Contoured	Segmented	Contoured
5–6 years	87	31	85	27
7–8 years	24	103	29	86
9–10 years	4	95	10	108

depiction of a clothed figure; the second is in the more realistic depiction of the limbs. In a very general sense, these findings lend support to Fenson's claim that children strive towards producing more realistic figures.

Partial Occlusion of Body Parts

It is difficult to know at what age children regard the outline of a figure or a particular body part as an *occluding contour* (see Chapter 1) in the sense that the figure is seen against its background from a specific viewpoint. Although the outline of the figure obviously defines it as a separate entity, the young child has not necessarily considered the figure from a particular viewpoint, taking into account what parts of the figure could or could not be seen from that viewpoint and the apparent shape of those parts that would be visible.

Perhaps a less ambiguous use of an occluding contour can be gauged when children draw one body part so that it appears to be in front of or behind another part; in other words, their depiction of *partial occlusion*. One example is an arm drawn across the figure's torso, so that part of the torso is masked from view. Sometimes the outline of the arm may be enclosed within the outline of the torso, but in other cases it may interrupt the contour of the torso, thereby giving a very clear effect of the partial occlusion of the torso. Among the figures drawn by my 5- to 6-year-olds, there were only three such cases in all (see Table 3.4): one child in the standard condition presented a frontal view of the figure but used the partial occlusion technique in which the arms appeared to partially occlude the sides of the upper torso, and two children in the running condition who drew profile figures drew the visible arm within the contour of the torso.

It seems intuitively likely that the ability to produce a partial occlusion would depend on a child's being able to adopt a particular point of view *vis-à-vis* the object to be drawn and, in imagining a figure in profile, being able to understand that the arm nearer the viewer will obscure part of the torso. In Piaget and Inhelder's (1956) account of the child's development of spatial concepts, they argue that this ability to adopt a viewpoint does not begin until about the age of 7 years, although it has been demonstrated that children in some circumstances can adopt a particular viewpoint at an earlier age (e.g. Cox, 1991) and, indeed, can produce a partial occlusion in their drawings (Cox, 1981; 1985). Piaget and Inhelder (1956) used the ideas and data from Luquet's (1913; 1927) work on children's drawing to support their case. Luquet himself had described the child's modifications of his drawings as a shift from intellectual to visual realism, that is from a concern with depicting what is known about an object to a concern with depicting it as it would appear from a particular viewpoint.

As one would predict from both Piaget and Inhelder's (1956) and Luquet's (1913; 1927) accounts, the number of occlusions increased among the older children I tested (see Table 3.4). In the standard condition at age 7–8 years, there were two drawings in each of the categories already mentioned and one in a third (3.9% in all) in which the figure was drawn so that its hand appeared to be behind its back. In the standard condition at age 9–10 years, there were 21 cases in all (21%). Not surprisingly, the running condition elicited more occlusions and most cases involved the limbs, particularly the arms, and the torso; there were 31 cases overall (27%) among the 7- to 8-year-olds and 69 (58%) among the 9- to 10-year-olds. Examples of the different kinds of occlusions are shown in Fig. 3.1. The emergence of the use of lines as occluding contours appears to be very closely related to the depiction of the figure in profile. Among the children in the two younger age groups drawing occlusions, 30 (77%) of them also drew the figure in profile.

Of course, these data are only indicative of what children at these different ages *choose* to draw; it is possible that more of them would have depicted partial occlusions if they had been presented with a model in which the partial occlusion of, say, the torso by an arm was very evident.

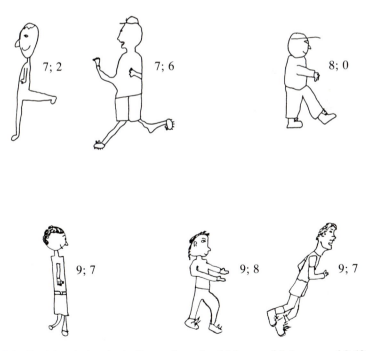

FIG. 3.1   Partial occlusions in the figures drawn by children aged 7–8 years and 9–10 years.

TABLE 3.4
Frequency of Partial Occlusions Within Figures Drawn by Children of Three Age Levels
in Two Conditions

	Age Group					
	5–6 years		7–8 years		9–10 years	
	Standard (n = 118)	Running (n = 112)	Standard (n = 127)	Running (n = 115)	Standard (n = 99)	Running (n = 118)
Arms						
Within torso outline		2	2	9	6	15
Interrupting torso outline	1		2	6	8	26
Arm/hand behind torso			1			
Short arm occluded by torso				6		10
Arm occluded by arm				4	1	7
Arm behind head						1
Others						
Hair/torso				2	2	
Beard/torso					1	
Ears/hair					1	
Leg/leg				4	2	10

None the less, one would still expect an age trend for at least two reasons. First, young children do not necessarily attend carefully to a model, even when their attention has been drawn to it (Barrett & Light, 1976; Cox & Nieland, cited in Cox, 1991, p. 81). And, secondly, it often takes a considerable amount of planning to avoid a transparency drawing and produce a partial occlusion, and this ability in itself appears to improve with age (Cox, 1992).

The Canonical View

The figures in young children's drawings have a characteristic stance: they face the viewer with legs apart and arms held away from the torso. This typical arrangement is often regarded as the *canonical* orientation of the figure (Dziurawiec and Derȩgowski, 1992; Freeman, 1980; Hochberg, 1972), the one which perhaps most clearly displays all the salient and defining features of a person. Although back views and side views are also feasible representations of the human form and in some circumstances might be regarded as a more correct depiction of what a viewer can see, nevertheless one might regard them as less satisfactory, since some of the criterial features of a person will be missing.

Rarely is it the case that the canonical view is even a veridical view since, usually, not all the features are drawn from one particular viewpoint. Typically, the feet, for example, are turned to the sides, pointing in opposite directions. Thus, although at first glance the figure as a whole appears to be drawn in a unified perspective, it is often in mixed profile.

Adults, as well as children, frequently choose to present a frontal view of the human form. In a sample of 46 adults' drawings, I found that the figures in 40 of them were frontal views, 5 were in profile and one was a back view. Adults, however, are more likely than children to maintain the frontal view for all the features of the figure, by foreshortening the feet for instance rather than turning them to the sides.

As well as displaying the criterial features of the human figure, the canonical view can also more easily indicate that each feature occupies its own space. This is difficult to achieve with a side view, because part or all of one arm may be occluded by the torso and the contour of the arm nearer the viewer usually cuts across the outline of the torso. In fact, Goodnow (1977, pp. 50–54) has argued that children strive to ensure that each body part has its own space and are very reluctant to overlap the boundaries. She illustrated this point by asking tadpole-drawers to add arms to some figures in which the hair already occupied the space where the arms normally go. The children rarely drew the arms across the hair but pointed them downwards or shifted them onto the legs of the figure. In my collection of standard figures drawn by children in three age groups, I also found that the overlap of one part by another was quite rare: among the 5- to 6-year-olds there were 11 cases (9%), among the 7- to 8-year-olds 6 cases (5%) and among the 9- to 10-year-olds 3 cases (3%). In most cases, the hair had encroached upon the torso or the outline of clothing had been superimposed on the limb or torso contours.

In general, it seems to be true that young children prefer to give each body part its own space. As well as the dearth of overlapping of one body part by another, there are also few cases of occlusions in the standard figure drawings of children below the age of 9 years. Older children and adults, however, are more likely to draw their figures with some body parts crossing others; nevertheless, they do this not by overlapping the contours of each part, but by depicting the occlusion of the farther by the nearer part from the viewer's perspective.

Figures in Profile

What constitutes a profile figure is not as straightforward as at first it might seem. In order to judge that a figure has been drawn in profile, should we demand that all the body parts are drawn in profile, or only some of them, or will just one of them suffice? Are some parts more definitive of a profile than others? And what are we to make of those figures in which one body part seems to point in one direction and another part points the opposite way?

In my study of children's standard human figure drawings at three different age levels, I first decided to classify a figure as being in profile if it showed any of the following body parts in profile: legs/feet, arms, head, and torso. In fact as I expected, the number of profile figures among the 5- to 6-year-olds was very low (14%; see Table 3.5). It was also the case, however, that the numbers were quite low among the two older groups: 17% at 7–8 years and 21% at 9–10 years. I considered that one of the main reasons for this low occurrence was that in the standard "draw a person" task, children are more concerned to draw the most detailed and recognisable figure they can, and this usually means that they choose to draw a canonical figure. It is more likely that children will choose to draw a profile figure if they are asked to draw a person in action. When I examined the pictures of another set of children who had been asked to draw a person running (see Table 3.5), I found an increase in the frequency of profile figures; nevertheless, although most children in the two older groups drew profiles (70 and 84%, respectively), just over half (57%) of the youngest group presented a frontal view.

At the youngest age, the feet were the most common body part drawn in profile; the arms and head were increasingly drawn in profile by the older children, but although the arms were drawn so as to give the impression of a side view of the figure, the shape of the torso itself was rarely altered—there were only two cases among the 7- to 8-year-olds and 11 among the 9- to 10-year olds.

It has been claimed that most profile figures point to the left (Guillaumin, 1961). Among my data, however, there is no support for this claim (see Table 3.6): When considering the feet, arms and head, either there is no difference in direction (among the 7- to 8-year-olds) or there is a preference for right-facing profiles (among the youngest and the oldest

TABLE 3.5
Frequency of Frontal and Profile Figures Drawn by Children of Three Age Levels in Two Conditions

	Standard		Running	
Age Group	Frontal	Profile	Frontal	Profile
5–6 years	102	16	65	47
7–8 years	105	22	34	81
9–10 years	78	21	19	99

TABLE 3.6
Frequency of Children in Three Age Levels Pointing the Feet, Arms or Head of Their Figures to the Left or to the Right

Age Group	Feet		Arms		Head	
	Left	*Right*	*Left*	*Right*	*Left*	*Right*
5–6 years	18	40	7	14	3	14
7–8 years	42	48	21	22	29	28
9–10 years	49	63	29	47	37	56

groups). Among the 13 cases of torsos drawn in profile, 8 faced to the left and 5 faced to the right. Since there was no significant difference in the direction of orientation between the standard and the running conditions, the data were combined.

The same criticism can be made here as that regarding the low frequency of occlusion in young children's drawings: Because the children were not asked specifically to draw a figure in profile, we cannot know whether they were unable to do so or whether they had simply chosen not to do so. In order to get a better idea of their abilities, one of my students, Rachel Moore, carried out a study in which three groups of conventional drawers aged 3–5 years ($n = 33$), 6 years ($n = 15$) and 8 years ($n = 15$) were shown a figure in its canonical orientation and in profile, and were asked to draw the two views.

All of the children drew a frontal view when the figure faced them, although four of the youngest children omitted the facial features. When the children saw a side view of the figure, 15 of the youngest ones drew a frontal view including the facial features and 3 of the children who had omitted the facial features for the canonical view omitted them again for the side view. The remaining 15 children in this youngest group made various attempts to modify their drawing to indicate a profile. These ranged from omitting the facial features (three cases), drawing only one eye (three cases), drawing only one leg (four cases) and drawing only one arm (four cases). There was no occlusion or overlapping of body parts among the youngest children's drawings.

Among the 6-year-olds, all but one made some attempt to modify their drawing when confronted with the figure in profile. Most of them orientated the feet to the side (11 cases) and drew one arm (11 cases), and 7 children modified the head or facial features. The arm occluded the torso in two cases and was enclosed within the contour of the torso in seven other cases. Among the 8-year-olds, all of them made adjustments to the face, arms and feet. One child occluded the contour of the torso with the arm; all of the others enclosed the arm within the torso's contour.

These data indicate that by the age of about 5 years, many children can make adjustments to their figures and take account of a profile view, and by the age of 6 years all of them can make at least one adjustment.

Figures in Action

Placing a figure, or parts of it, in profile is one way of indicating that the figure is in action. But there are other ways, too, as Goodnow's (1977; 1978) studies of children's drawings of figures walking and running show. Among the 5- to 10-year-olds she tested, the youngest children showed the least adaptation of their figures, usually simply placing the legs of the running figure at a wider angle than those of the walking figure. These findings are echoed in a study by Papadakis-Michaelides (1989), who also found that the action figures drawn by most children between 4 years 6 months and 6 years 5 months were not in fact different from their normal human figure drawings, even though the children claimed some task or action for them. With increasing age, the children in Goodnow's studies altered the positioning or the "give" in the legs and also the arms of their figures. The adaptation of the torso was found almost exclusively among the 9- to 10-year-olds. Goodnow argued that children are at first able to alter only the peripheral or accessory parts of the figure (the legs, arms or facial features) and not until much later in development are they able to adapt the "core" of the figure (i.e. the torso).

In my study, the children in the running figure group were different from those in the standard group, so it was not possible to compare the running figures with those same children's normal figures. Nevertheless, I did find that among the running figures drawn by my 5- to 6-year-olds, there were 13 cases in which the angle between the legs seemed particularly exaggerated. Other devices children used to indicate action were: a bent leg or a leg "up in the air" ($n = 13$), one arm bent ($n = 2$), torso leaning to one side ($n = 1$), multiple legs to indicate movement ($n = 1$) and "lines for speed" added behind a profile figure ($n = 1$). The incidence of these devices increased among my older samples, although the adaptation of the torso was not particularly frequent: four cases among the 7- to 8-year-olds and eight among the 9- to 10-year-olds.

It does not seem unreasonable, however, that the torso of a running figure should remain in a fairly upright position. And it was for this reason that Goodnow asked children to draw a figure bending down to pick up a ball. In this case, it seems almost obligatory that the torso should be bent. Again, she found that it was the youngest children who showed the least adaptation of their figures, often drawing a canonical view with the ball either on the ground or placed higher up on the page adjacent to a hand. Although slightly older children also tended to leave their basic figures intact, they might elongate one of the arms so that it reached down to the ball or might lean the whole figure over to one side. It was only the older children (from age 8 years upwards) who made more radical alterations to the structure of their figures: At first, they bent the figures at the waist, so that they resembled an inverted "V"; later, they also bent the legs at the knees, thereby creating a much more realistic and less rigid impression.

Transparency Drawings

Transparency drawings are defined as those in which something in the drawing can be seen which in reality would be impossible. They tend to fall into two types. In one, the figure has the appearance of a cross-section in which the "invisible" parts—perhaps the food in someone's stomach or a baby in the womb—are usually enclosed by the contour of the torso. I have argued elsewhere (Cox, 1992) that these kinds of transparency drawings are not mistakes; on the contrary, the children have deliberately drawn the parts which are normally invisible. Usually they do not need to alter their normal schema for the figure except perhaps to make the torso segment larger in order to accommodate its extra contents. A second type of transparency is probably the result of an error or a lack of foresight in planning. Examples include when a child draws the torso of a figure and then clothes it or draws the outline of the torso and then draws the arm across it. In these cases, the child does not intend the torso to be seen.

In children's standard drawings of the human figure, transparencies actually occur rather infrequently. In the data I have discussed already in the section on canonicality, there were very few cases. Similarly, among my sample of 330 conventional-drawers with an average age of 5 years 6 months, there were only six transparencies: in one, the food was shown inside the figure's stomach; in another, the line of the figure's chin could be seen through its beard; and in the four other cases, the limbs and torsos of the figures could be seen through their clothing. Mann and Lehman (1976) also noted relatively low instances of transparencies in standard drawings of the human figure. Even when they tried to elicit them by asking 4- to 9-year-olds to draw a woman wearing a long skirt or a man wearing a coat, they still found that the frequency was not particularly high (i.e. 33%).

I have already discussed one reason why transparency drawings may be relatively rare and that is that young children are reluctant to overlap different body parts. Another reason, which may well have operated in Mann and Lehman's study, is that by the age of about 5–6 years, many children have developed a way of drawing the human figure which gives the impression that it is clothed; they do not draw a basic figure and then put the clothes on it, but build up the figure with contoured units which give the appearance of items of clothing, such as a jumper or jacket, trousers, etc.

There are far more transparencies among children's drawings of more unusual views of the human figure—in particular, when the body is seen in profile with the arm, for example, occluding part of the torso. And we have already seen, in the section on children's profile drawings, how one strategy for dealing with this view is to draw the torso first and then the contour of the arm across it.

Bodily Proportions

Children's conventional figures are generally taller than they are wide, reflecting to this extent at least the proportions of real people. In fact, as early as 1904, Schuyten noted that with increasing age children do manage to approximate the true proportions of the human figure. Nevertheless, their proportions often strike one as unrealistic. In particular, the head is often drawn much larger in proportion to the torso than it ought to be (Arnheim, 1974; Freeman, 1980; Goodenough, 1926; Harris, 1963; Nash & Harris, 1970). In the adult male, the ratio of head height to overall body height is 1:8 (Nash & Harris, 1970) and the ratio of head to torso height is 1:6 (Selfe, 1983).

It's possible that the head's overshadowing proportions may result from it having been drawn first and therefore having first choice of the available space (Freeman, 1980; Major, 1906). In order to test this hypothesis, Selfe (1983) asked children to draw a head onto a pre-drawn torso and found that 5- to 6-year-olds in particular drew the head much smaller than normal. A problem with Selfe's study, identified by Thomas and Tsalimi (1988), is that the pre-drawn torso had a neck and a rather narrow neck at that. Since 5- to 6-year-olds rarely draw necks on their figures, it may have been their preoccupation with how they should fix the head onto the neck that resulted in their drawing smaller heads.

Thomas and Tsalimi compared the sizes of heads drawn onto four different kinds of torso displaying (a) the neck used by Selfe, (b) an equally narrow but collarless neck, (c) a wide neck and (d) no neck. They found that their 3- to 4-year-olds and 5- to 6-year-olds did indeed draw smaller heads onto Selfe's torso and also onto the other narrow-neck torso too; the heads drawn onto the wide-neck and no-neck torsos were larger. However, among the 5- to 6-year-olds and 7- to 8-year-olds, the heads drawn onto the no-neck torso were actually more realistically proportioned than those in these children's free drawings. Of course, in this experiment they were asked to add the head to a torso, whereas in their free drawings they usually drew the head first and then the torso.

Thus, in a second experiment, Thomas and Tsalimi asked half their 5-to 6-year-olds and 7- to 8-year-olds to draw a man beginning with the head first and the other half beginning with the torso first. When the head was drawn first the children tended to overestimate it, whereas when the body was drawn first the proportions of the figure were more accurate. Interestingly, when the torso was drawn first the children always left room for the head, but when the head was drawn first 19% of the younger and 21% of the older children had not left enough space, thereby forcing them to draw the torso smaller in relation to the head. As was the case in the first experiment, the proportions of the figure were more realistic when the torso was drawn first. We have evidence from these studies, then, that children overestimate the size of the head when it is drawn first.

A second hypothesis relating to the oversized head has been suggested by Freeman (1980), namely that the head usually includes more details than the torso and that children anticipate this by exaggerating the size of the head segment. In order to test this hypothesis, Henderson and Thomas (1990) first asked children aged from 4 to 7 years to draw a man. They then divided the children among four conditions and asked one group to draw a man showing his teeth, a second group to draw a man showing his "jacket with bright shiny buttons and big pockets", a third group to draw the back of a man "so that you cannot see his face", and a fourth group to draw the twin brother of their first man so that he looked exactly the same as the first. This last condition provided baseline data regarding the change in proportions when children are asked to draw two figures one after the other; in fact, it was found that there was no significant change in head:torso ratio from one figure to the next.

The researchers compared the proportions of the children's second drawings with those in their first standard figure and then compared the head:torso proportions of the figures in the three experimental conditions against those in the twin condition. Although the heads in the teeth condition were relatively larger, the difference was not significant. It was suggested that this might have been either because the children did not think that teeth would take up much space and therefore did not require a particularly large head, or because the head size had already been expanded to a "ceiling" level. At least the first of these suggestions could be tested by varying the amount of detail to be included in the head segment; one could, for example, ask children to draw a man, showing his teeth, glasses, a beard and a moustache. Whereas the size of the head in Henderson and Thomas's study was not increased as much as had been expected, the torsos in the jacket condition were significantly larger and, finally, in the back-view condition the size of the head was significantly reduced. In a similar study, Willatts and Dougal (n.d.) confirmed that

3- to 10-year-old children draw the head of a figure much larger when it is viewed from the front than from the back.

Some authors, such as Thomas and Tsalimi (1988), have concluded from their studies that the proportions of children's figures are mainly the result of the planning involved in the construction of the drawings. Their findings certainly support the hypothesis that children can, and perhaps often do, anticipate the amount of detail to be included in the head or torso segments and then draw relatively large or small segments accordingly. Since children normally add more details in the head segment than in the torso, the head will tend to be drawn disproportionately large.

In contrast, a number of other writers have claimed that the head is drawn relatively large compared with other body parts because it is the most important part of the human figure (e.g. Di Leo, 1973; Lark-Horovitz et al., 1973; Löwenfeld, 1939). In fact, these views need not be incompatible. Without denying that children are indeed engaged in a planning exercise when they draw the human figure, we might speculate nevertheless that their decision to draw the head first and to include more details in it may be because they regard it as the most important and perhaps as the most defining part of the human figure (see Chapter 2).

Representational Redescription

I have presented a body of evidence in this chapter that children in the middle years of childhood are increasingly able to extend and adapt their earlier, somewhat minimal and rigid drawings. For Karmiloff-Smith (1986; 1990), such evidence supports her general theory of the shift from the efficiently functioning but constrained thinking of the younger child to the greater cognitive flexibility of the older child. She describes how a young child of, say, 4–6 years has developed an adequate and well-practised schema for the human figure—what Luquet (1913; 1927) called *type constancy*—and argues that this schema is guided by the application of a rigid, sequential procedure which is not amenable to modification. This means that the child is unable to interrupt the procedure in order to add to or modify the body parts she is drawing. Additions or modifications, if they are made at all, must be carried out at the beginning or at the end of the main procedure. Older children, say from the age of about 8 years, are no longer constrained to go through the procedure as a whole from beginning to end; they are able to carry out the procedure in a different order, delete parts of it, or add parts into it.

The evidence for Karmiloff-Smith's position comes from her study of 54 4- to 10-year-olds who were asked to draw a man and a man "who does not exist" (also a real animal and a house and an animal and a house which do not exist). All of the children drew adequate drawings of the real objects and 91% of the 4- to 6-year-olds and 94% of the 8- to 10-year-olds succeeded in drawing non-existent men and a non-existent house (the animal category was more problematic). The important issue concerns the kinds of changes that the children made in the "non-existent" drawings. Most of the changes made by the younger children were changes in shape of particular elements in their normal schema or to the general shape of it. The children were also able to delete certain elements but, according to Karmiloff-Smith, these were elements normally drawn at the end of the procedure. Very few of these younger children added an extra element to the drawing but, of those who did, all of them did so after they had finished the normal drawing procedure. In contrast, the older children altered their normal schemas in a greater variety of ways and also made deletions, additions or alterations during the course of the drawing procedure.

Karmiloff-Smith has argued that in order to bring about these modifications, the child needs to redescribe the procedures she is using; the earlier, fixed, sequentially ordered list is redescribed as a spatial structure whose elements can be considered and manipulated separately. Attractive though this argument is, it is based on the assumption that the sequential order of the elements in a child's drawing is very rigid. Although data from cross-sectional studies show that body parts *tend* to be added to children's human figure drawings in an orderly way (head, body, legs, arms), not all children adopt this sequence and evidence from longitudinal studies show that individual children do not always adhere to the same order for all of their figures. This suggests, then, that if children do have a sequential procedure for producing a schema, there is some flexibility in it from the beginning.

Further criticism of Karmiloff-Smith's position comes from studies of children's human figure drawings carried out by Spensley (1990). She repeated Karmiloff-Smith's man and non-existent man tasks and also asked children to draw a man with a beard. In contrast to Karmiloff-Smith's results, Spensley found that 4- to 6-year-olds were able to make alterations to their figures "mid-procedure". She repeated the tasks with even younger children—eight nursery children aged between 3 years 6 months and 4 years 11 months—and again found that all of them made at least some of their modifications mid-procedure. The evidence presented by Spensley, as well as that reported in Chapter 2 concerning the tadpole-drawers' ability to construct a manikin figure, suggests that younger children's simpler and seemingly more stereotyped figures are not simply the result of a rigid procedure which they are unable to alter. The production process appears to be much more flexible and accessible than the "procedural" account implies.

An alternative explanation already prevalent in the literature is that children increasingly seek more realistic forms of representation (Golomb, 1981; Goodnow, 1977; Luquet, 1913; 1927), adding more and more items which are clearly recognisable and, then, attempting to make the figure more visually realistic as seen from a particular viewpoint.

Summary

By the age of about 5–6 years, most children draw a conventional figure and include in it the main body parts—head, torso, arms and legs. They continue adding further details to their figures until the age of about 12 years. At first, the extra body parts are added as separate items, each with its own line or boundary giving the figure a segmented appearance. Later, some parts, noticeably the arms and the torso or the legs and the torso, are unified by a continuous contour giving the figure a more fluid appearance. This contouring effect may be prompted by the child's intention to construct the figure with units depicting items of clothing, such as a jumper and some trousers.

When children—and indeed adults—are simply asked to "draw a person", they prefer to present the figure in its canonical orientation, facing the viewer and with little overlap of body parts. With these instructions, profile figures are quite rare. When children are shown a model in profile and are asked to draw it, most 6-year-olds and even many 5-year-olds make some attempt to modify the figure. Nevertheless, it is only at a later stage that children use the technique of occlusion to indicate that, for example, a part of the torso is masked by an arm from the viewer's perspective.

The heads of young children's figures are disproportionately large and some researchers and clinicians have argued that this reflects the importance that the head has relative to the other body parts. Whether or not this is true, other researchers have shown that the disproportionate size of the head is related to the fact that it is usually drawn first and also that it needs to contain a number of facial details. When these variables have been experimentally manipulated, children are capable of drawing figures with more realistic proportions. It may be, then, that the typically disproportionate figures are the result of production problems rather than the psychological meaningfulness of particular body parts, most notably the head.

Although it has been suggested that the child becomes more adept at modifying her figures because she becomes more able to review and manipulate the procedure she uses for producing the schema, the empirical evidence does not provide support for this argument. It seems that even quite young children are not necessarily constrained to produce their figures in a fixed way and, when required, are quite adept at making modifications to their normal procedures. Nevertheless, some of their difficulties (e.g. transparency figures) may result from problems in planning the sequence of the figure and their mastery of this appears to be developmentally related.

4 Human Figure Drawings as Measures of Intellectual Maturity

Early Investigations

Some early investigators of children's human figure drawings such as Schuyten (1904) and Lobsien (1905) noted that with a child's increasing chronological age, the number of body parts in the figure increased and the proportions of the body parts became more realistic. Rouma (1913) observed that these changes in children's human figure drawings were even more strongly related to their increasing mental age than to chronological age. Although attempts were made to use these aspects of human figure drawings to establish a set of age norms for use as an indicator of a child's general level of intellectual ability, it was to be another 20 years before such a project was successful.

The Draw-a-Man Test

The Draw-a-Man test was developed by Goodenough (1926), who selected 51 details of the human figure for attention. Children were asked to draw "a picture of a man. Make the very best picture that you can" (p. 85). Each child's drawing was then credited with points according to the number of body parts drawn, their proportions and the way that the parts were attached to the main figure.

The girl (aged 5 years 9 months) who drew the man in Fig. 4.1 (Goodenough, 1926, p. 122, fig. 22) gained points for having drawn a head, containing eyes, nose (nostrils) and mouth. The figure also has hair. A torso is present and is longer than it is broad. Legs and arms are attached

Girl, Jewish, age 5–9, kindergarten. Credits, 1, 2, 3,
4 a, 4 b, 5 a, 7 a, 7 b, 7 c, 7 e, 8 a, 9 a, 10 e, 12 a, 12 b. Total
score 15. M.A. 6–9. IQ 117.

FIG. 4.1 Credits and IQ scores gained in the Draw-a-Man test by a girl aged 5 years 9
months. (From Goodenough, 1926.)

to the torso and the figure has hands. There is evidence of clothing and
both the head and the arms of the figure are well-proportioned. The figure
is credited with a total of 15 points, which Goodenough then converted to
an IQ score—in this case, 117 (see Goodenough, 1926, p. 123).

The drawing of a man by a boy aged 11 years 2 months shown in Fig.
4.2 scored 47 points (Goodenough, 1926, p. 132, fig. 39). Not only are
there more body parts compared with the 5-year-old's figure shown in Fig.
4.1—for instance, a neck, ears, fingers and heels—and more detailed
clothing, but the proportions of the figure are better and the control and
co-ordination of the lines is more confident. The figure is also drawn in
profile. When the points are converted though, the figure has an IQ score
of 116. Like the 5-year-old, this boy also scored above average for his age.

Reliability of the Draw-a-Man Test

Goodenough (1926) reported a correlation of 0.937 between figures
completed on 2 successive days by 194 7-year-olds. A number of other
researchers have also checked the reliability of the Draw-a-Man test:
McCarthy (1944), for example, tested 386 children in the third and fourth

Boy, Armenian, age 11-2, low fifth grade. Credits,
1, 2, 3, 4 a, 4 b, 4 c, 5 a, 5 b, 6 a, 6 b, 7 a, 7 b, 7 c, 7 d, 7 e, 8 a, 8 b,
9 a, 9 b, 9 c, 9 d, 9 e, 10 a, 10 b, 11 a, 11 b, 12 a, 12 b, 12 c, 12 e,
13, 14 a, 14 b, 14 c, 14 d, 14 e, 14 f, 15 a, 16 a, 16 b, 16 c, 16 d, 17 a,
17 b, 18 a, 18 b. Total score 47. M.A. 13–0 or above. IQ 116
or above.

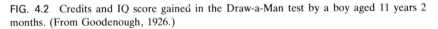

FIG. 4.2 Credits and IQ score gained in the Draw-a-Man test by a boy aged 11 years 2
months. (From Goodenough, 1926.)

grades twice with an inter-test interval of 1 week and found a correlation
of 0.94 when the drawings were scored by the same scorers on both
occasions and 0.90 when scored by different scorers. Yepsen (1929) found
a similarly high test–retest correlation of 0.90 using "feeble-minded"
subjects. McCurdy's (1947) correlation of 0.69, however, based on the
drawings of 56 first-grade children, was lower but still significant. In a study
by Williams (1935), the inter-rater reliability correlations of five examiners
scoring 100 drawings ranged from 0.80 to 0.96. Harris (1963) found the
variation to be "quite insignificant" when he examined the scores of four
groups of kindergarten children tested by Goodenough (1926) on each of
10 successive days.

In general, then, the reliability of the test appears to be reasonably high.
There are, nevertheless, some dissenting reports, such as that by Griffiths
(1945, p. 218), who found that the assessed mental age of one girl aged 3
years 10 months varied from 3 years 9 months to 4 years 6 months during
a 20-day period. Kellogg (1969, p. 191) also reported great variability in

the way that one-third of a sample of 2500 children drew their human figures over a 5-day period; although she did not report any further details, she claimed that the scores of these children varied as much as 50%.

Validity of the Draw-a-Man Test

Estimates of the validity of the test are much more variable. According to Harris's (1963) review, correlations between the Draw-a-Man test and other tests of intelligence vary considerably (from 0.20 to 0.80) depending on the age range of the subjects and the age range included in the sample. Goodenough (1926) correlated the drawing IQs and Stanford-Binet IQs (Terman, 1916) of children aged between 4 and 10 years: the lowest correlation was 0.699 for the 5-year-olds and the highest was 0.863 for the 4-year-olds. Yepsen's (1929) correlation was 0.60, Williams's (1935) was 0.65, and using 14-year-old retarded children as subjects McElwee's (1932) was 0.72 between the Draw-a-Man test and the Stanford-Binet test.

The Revised Drawing Test

By the time Harris (1963) revised the Draw-a-Man test, extending the list to 71 items, both he and Goodenough had come to regard it as a measure of intellectual and conceptual maturity and not of intelligence, in that the test supposedly measures the child's actual rather than his potential level. The revised test does not yield a score identical with IQ, even though, according to Harris, the correlations between IQ and drawing scores are quite substantial for children between the ages of 5 and 10 years.

The notion of conceptual maturity, according to Harris, concerns the ability to perceive and discriminate similarities and differences, the ability to abstract these and the ability to generalise or classify objects correctly. The child's drawing of an object is an index of his concept of that object, and his concept of a frequently experienced object such as a human being is a useful index of the growing complexity of his concepts in general.

Girls tend to add more details to their figures than do boys of the same age, thereby gaining more points on average on the Draw-a-Man test. This superiority may reflect the generally faster maturation rate of girls (Scott, 1981). In order to compensate for this in the Draw-a-Man test, there are separate tables for boys and girls for converting their total points to standard scores.

The revised test also requires children to make three drawings (a man, a woman and a self-drawing) and provides separate norms for drawings of males and females. Harris (1963, p. 107) advised that in assessing intellectual maturity, the scores from a child's male and female figures should be averaged in order to give a more accurate estimate of achievement than can be gained from a single figure alone.

Koppitz's Developmental Items

Another mental test based on children's drawings of the human figure was developed by Koppitz (1968), based on the human figure drawings of nearly 2000 children aged between 5 and 12 years. She scored each figure according to 30 *developmental items* derived from the Goodenough–Harris test and from her own experience of studying children's drawings (see Table 4.1). These developmental items were grouped into four categories for each age level: (1) expected, (2) common, (3) not unusual and (4) exceptional. Legs, for example, are expected items in a 6-year-old's figure. If a 6-year-old has drawn legs, then he scores +1; if the legs are absent, then a score of −1 is recorded. Exceptional features will occur only in the figures of children with above-average mental maturity. As in the Goodenough–Harris Draw-a-Man test, a child's total score can be converted into an IQ score. There is a positive and significant correlation between the number of developmental items on Koppitz's test and the score on a standard IQ test (Koppitz, 1968, pp. 30–31). She reports a correlation of 0.63 with the Stanford-Binet test (Terman & Merrill, 1960) at ages 6 and 7 years and 0.62 at ages 11 and 12 years; correlations with the Wechsler Intelligence Scale for Children (WISC; Wechsler, 1967) range from 0.60 at ages 6 and 7 years to 0.80 at age 12 years.

TABLE 4.1
The 30 Developmental Items in Koppitz's Draw-a-Person Test

1. Head	16. Arms correctly attached to shoulders
2. Eyes	17. Elbows
3. Pupils	18. Hands
4. Eyebrows or eyelashes	19. Fingers
5. Nose	20. Correct number of fingers
6. Nostrils	21. Legs
7. Mouth	22. Legs in two dimensions
8. Two lips	23. Knees
9. Ears	24. Feet
10. Hair	25. Feet in two dimensions
11. Neck	26. Profile
12. Body	27. Clothing: one item or none
13. Arms	28. Clothing: two or three items
14. Arms in two dimensions	29. Clothing: four or more items
15. Arms pointing downwards	30. Good proportions

Children with Learning Difficulties

In 1913 Rouma, who had included "feeble-minded" as well as normal subjects in his study, claimed that children with learning difficulties (LD) produce the same kinds of drawings that normal children produce, albeit at a younger age. In other words, the standard of children's drawings is closer to their mental age than to their chronological age. This idea suggests that children with learning difficulties are not producing figures which are particularly aberrant, but are simply proceeding through the "stages" of drawing at a slower pace than normal children. A number of other researchers, however, such as Schuyten (1904), Kerschensteiner (1905), Lobsien (1905), Burt (1921) and Goodenough (1926), claimed that there are noticeable differences between the drawings of LD and normal children. Interestingly, it seems that the LD children may well include more details in their figures than normals of the same mental age, but it is the unusual proportions of the figures which is a particular characteristic of LD children (Earl, 1933; Israelite, 1936; McElwee, 1934; Spoerl, 1940).

Because these early studies suffered from a variety of methodological shortcomings, Golomb and Barr-Grossman (1977) argued that it was not possible to establish which view is more likely. These authors compared the human figure drawings of children with non-specific learning difficulties (chronological age 4 years 4 months to 13 years 1 month; IQ 40–76) with those of normal children (chronological age 3 years to 5 years 10 months; IQ approximately 100–110). The mental age of the LD group was similar to that of a comparison group of normal children, although of course the normal children were younger. Although they give no illustrative examples of the figures drawn by the children, Golomb and Barr-Grossman say that the structure of the figures drawn by the two groups was very similar; the only difference was that the LD children with a mental age of 4 and 5 years drew more details than did the normal children of that age. Apart from this difference, the drawings were remarkably similar, with no noticeable problems of organisation, proportion or addition of bizarre details.

The findings of a study by Cox and Howarth (1989), like those of Golomb and Barr-Grossman (1977), also suggest that children with learning difficulties exhibit a developmental delay in the structuring of their figures rather than a disorder or deviance in their drawing ability. Cox and Howarth's group of children with severe learning difficulties had an average chronological age of 9 years and 2 months, but their average mental age was 3 years 9 months. They compared the human figure drawings of these children with two groups of normal children: a primary school group which also had a mean chronological age of 9 years (mean mental age 7 years 8 months), and a younger nursery group (mean chronological age 4 years) whose mean mental age was similar to that of the

LD group (4 years 8 months). Each figure was categorised according to a 5-point classification devised by Cox and Parkin (1986): (1) scribbles, (2) shapes, (3) tadpole figures, (4) transitional figures and (5) conventional figures. Whereas all the children in the primary school group produced conventional figures, few of the LD children or the nursery children did so; in fact, the drawings of the LD and the nursery children were very similar and both groups produced less advanced drawings than the normal 9-year-olds (see Fig. 4.3). Furthermore, both the LD and the nursery children showed the body-proportion effect (Freeman, 1975; see also Chapter 2), whereas the primary children did not.

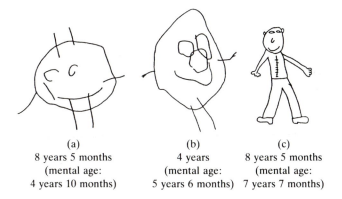

(a)	(b)	(c)
8 years 5 months	4 years	8 years 5 months
(mental age:	(mental age:	(mental age:
4 years 10 months)	5 years 6 months)	7 years 7 months)

FIG. 4.3   Human figure drawings by (a) a child with severe learning difficulties, (b) a nursery school child and (c) a primary school child. (Reproduced with the permission of Penguin Books Ltd.)

The findings from these studies suggest that the structure of the human figure drawings of children with learning difficulties is very similar to those of younger normal children matched for mental age; one difference, however, is that the LD children tend to add more details to their figures (a point also noted by earlier researchers of children's drawings), although not as many as do their chronological age controls.

Drawing the Best Picture

Whatever the administrator's intention regarding the scoring system to be used, it is extremely important that the instructions are adhered to when administering the test to the children. In particular, only those figure drawings which have been drawn on request should be scored. The reason for this is that these figures tend to be more detailed and better proportioned than those which children draw spontaneously for themselves. Goodnow, Wilkins, and Dawes (1986), using the Goodenough–Harris scoring system, found that a sample of 15 6-year-olds averaged a score of 12.5 ± 3.09 (SD) for their requested drawings compared with 11.68 ± 2.76 for their spontaneous figures. A group of 16 7-year-olds also showed this difference, averaging 15.27 ± 4.99 for requested drawings and 12.77 ± 4.71 for spontaneous figures. A further finding was that whereas these older children depicted stationary figures in their requested drawings, 69% of the spontaneous figures displayed action and these action figures were less detailed, more experimental and less practised. In fact, Goodenough and Harris (1950) themselves were at pains to emphasise the importance of gathering data under controlled conditions: "Many of the reputedly abnormal features in the drawings of single children or of small, selected groups lose their apparent significance when the age and sex of the subjects and the conditions under which the drawings were made become known" (p. 371).

Even when the administrator has collected data under carefully controlled conditions, he or she may none the less wish to be assured that the children's requested figure drawings are representative of their very best efforts. Such assurance may be gained by repeated testing and/or from a collection of the child's spontaneous drawings completed around the time of testing.

Yet a further note of caution, this time regarding the use of the Draw-a-Man test with LD children, comes from a study by Pollak (1986), who reviewed 18 published, empirical studies relevant to figure-drawing performance. Most of these studies used either the Goodenough–Harris or the Koppitz scoring systems. Pollak was investigating a claim, widespread among practitioners, that for children with learning difficulties, the IQ scores obtained from the Goodenough–Harris system are lower than those derived from some other standardised tests of cognitive functioning, thereby underestimating the children's abilities. He did, in fact, find modest support for this claim.

Summary

The use of children's human figure drawings as an indicator of their intelligence or intellectual maturity has a long history. Well-known scoring systems such as those devised by Goodenough and Harris and by Koppitz are reasonably reliable and valid. They have been used extensively with both normal children and those with learning difficulties. Despite early suggestions that LD children's drawings were qualitatively different from those drawn by normals, it is now considered that most LD children produce drawings similar in structure to those of their mental-age controls; any differences usually concern the number of details added to the figure and, on this score, LD children include more.

Human figure drawings collected under strictly controlled conditions can be used to give a reasonably good guide to a child's general intellectual level. They cannot, however, be used to assess particular kinds of difficulty and one would not recommend that important decisions about a child's treatment should rest on the results of this test alone.

In addition to the cautionary notes already sounded, it is important to emphasise that the use of the tests discussed in this chapter is appropriate only in those populations in which the reliability and validity of the tests have been assessed. It would make no sense to try to make estimates of intelligence or intellectual maturity among individuals in populations in which such checks have not been made. Furthermore, in Western societies, at least, the tests are based on an observed developmental progression, namely the increasing addition of body parts with age and adaptations towards more realistically shaped and proportioned figures. Again, if such a developmental progression is not observed or is not known in a particular population, then the test cannot be used in any meaningful way.

5 Human Figure Drawings as Indicators of Children's Personality and Emotional Adjustment

Writers such as Wolff (1946) became dissatisfied with the analysis of children's drawings purely from a cognitive-developmental point of view and argued that an important element had been omitted, namely the emotional factor. And indeed, there is no doubt in some people's minds that the activity of drawing, which appears to be so "natural" and "spontaneous", can be useful in providing a window on a child's general and basic nature (see review by Harris in Buros, 1972, pp. 401–404). It is as if the child cannot help but reveal her feelings through the medium of the picture.

The Machover Draw-a-Person Test

Machover's (1949) Draw-a-Person test has been considered to be a very useful way of assessing personality, being based on the assumptions that "the drawing of a person represents the expression of self, or the body, in the environment" (Machover, 1951, p. 348) and "the composite image that constitutes the figure drawn is intimately tied to the self in all of its ramifications" (p. 349). Distortions of the figure are deemed to be symbolic representations of inadequacies or distortions of the drawer's self-image, an argument also put forward or at least endorsed by several other researchers (e.g. Berman & Laffal, 1953; Buck, 1948; Schildkrout, Shenker, & Sonnenblick, 1972). First the child is asked to "draw a person" or to "draw somebody"; this figure is interpreted as an expression of self and sex-role identification. The child is then asked to draw a second figure on another sheet of paper; if the first figure was a male, then the examiner asks for a female figure, and vice versa. The second figure is interpreted as revealing something about the child's relationship to other important people in her life. Machover's interpretation of the drawings takes into account the particular body parts included, their size and shape, their position on the page, the quality of the line, the amount of erasure, and so on. The interpretation is heavily influenced by a psychoanalytic orientation, imbuing almost every line and segment of the drawing with symbolic meaning and taking no account of the way that perfectly normal young children draw.

Figure 5.1 shows a picture drawn by 8-year-old Peter, which Machover (1951) has used as an example to illustrate her method of personality analysis through the drawing of the human figure. Peter came from a middle-class family and he himself was of superior intelligence, was socially polite and had cultivated, adult manners. His father, a physician, had been overseas for 3 years and his mother had been distraught, unstable and restless during this time. She vacillated in her management of Peter, alternating between indulgence and harsh discipline. Peter had become increasingly aggressive, restless and attention-seeking by telling bawdy stories, swearing and handling his genitals.

When asked to draw a person, Peter placed his figure in the centre of the page. Machover considers that this male figure represents Peter himself and that its central location is another example of his attempts to force himself into the centre of attention. She also believes that, although the stance of the figure is wide and assertive, the shading and erasure on the chest area indicate a sense of weakness. The oversized head indicates intellectual aspiration and the heavy pressure of the pencil line indicates a need for social participation. The pronounced ears reflect an over-sensitivity to social opinion and criticism. The omission of the pupils from the eyes indicates self-centredness. The meticulous and manly clothing (the oversized tie in particular) indicates an accent on social appearances and a father replacement drive. Sexual anxiety and conflict are indicated by the extra shading on the trousers and the strong belt which cuts off the genital area. The small feet indicate insecurity and effeminacy.

When Peter was asked to draw a female, he at first attempted to draw on the reverse side of the page but then drew a figure close to his first one. Machover interprets this second figure as a representation of his mother and says that Peter must always be close to his mother physically and could not tolerate even graphic separation. When Machover asked Peter to talk about the figure in his picture, he said that the male figure is a boy aged 12 and that he is walking through the park with his sister, aged 11. Machover notes that Peter frequently walks in the nearby park with his mother and that the theme of walking may indicate a trend towards overactivity.

FIG. 5.1   A drawing by Peter, a normal child, used by Machover (1951) to illustrate her diagnostic technique.

Criticisms of the Machover Test

Swensen (1957) reviewed a great many studies which had used the test in order to assess Machover's claims but concluded that ". . . the evidence does not support Machover's hypotheses about the meaning of the human figure drawings. More of the evidence directly contradicts her hypotheses than supports them" (p. 460). Furthermore, "Since in clinical work the reliable diagnosis of the individual case is of paramount importance, this lack of consistent evidence . . . suggests that the DAP is of doubtful value in clinical work" (pp. 460–461). Some years later, Swensen (1968) and Roback (1968) reviewed the up-to-date evidence and both authors were essentially in agreement: they could not find sufficient evidence in support of Machover's claims.

As an example of the lack of consensus regarding Machover's claims, I will outline briefly some of the research relating to the size of the figure and the subject's own self-esteem. Machover (1949) claimed that the size of the figure, assumed to represent the subject himself, reflects his self-esteem. This view was supported by Hammer (1958), and Koppitz (1968) also noted that tiny figures reflect the subject's insecurity and timidity.

One problem in assessing research studies is the lack of any independent evidence for the subject's level of self-esteem. Gray and Pepitone (1964) tried to remedy this problem by experimentally manipulating the self-esteem of groups of male undergraduates. They found no relationship between these manipulations and the size of the students' human figure drawings. This is perhaps not surprising, since the researchers did not measure the subjects' normal levels of self-esteem, nor did they check whether their manipulations had been successful in creating different levels of self-esteem. The same criticism can be made against a study by McHugh (1963). Better controlled investigations were carried out by Bennett (1964), who tested 198 sixth-graders (aged 11–12 years) and found no relationship between self-esteem and size of figures. Similarly, Prytula and Thompson (1973) found no relationship among 10- to 13-year-olds.

Some researchers have used well-established tests in order to assess subjects' self-esteem. Dalby and Vale (1977), for example, gave the Coopersmith Self-esteem Inventory (Coopersmith, 1967) to 115 grade 5 children aged 10–11 years. The test requires subjects to respond "like me" or "unlike me" to 50 self-evaluative statements. Five teachers also rated the subjects' self-esteem on a scale of 1–5. In addition, the subjects were asked to draw themselves and two friends of the same age. Although the relationship between the two measures of self-esteem was significant, there was no association between the absolute height of the self-figures and each of the two measures of self-esteem.

One problem in studying self-esteem among children is that before adolescence the notion of "self" may be "ambiguous or vaguely formed" (Coopersmith, Sakai, Beardslee, & Coopersmith, 1976). For this reason, Delatte and Hendrickson (1982) used older subjects: 38 male and 38 female 16- to 18-year-olds. These authors also pointed out the lack of consensus in previous research over the meaning of "size" of the subjects' human figure drawings; in their own study, they took the precaution of measuring height, width and area of the figures. A further criticism of previous work concerned the hypothesised relationship between self-esteem and figure size. In line with Machover's psychoanalytic orientation, some subjects scoring low on self-esteem may draw tiny figures but others may over-compensate for their feelings and draw very large figures (Machover, 1949, p. 90). Thus, the relationship between self-esteem and size of figure drawing should be *curvilinear*. Delatte and Hendrickson (1982) did, in fact, find such a relationship between self-esteem (measured by the Rosenberg Self-esteem Scale: Rosenberg, 1965) and height and area of the drawings among these older teenagers, but only among their male subjects; there were no significant correlations at all for the females.

After reviewing a wide range of Machover's claims, Swensen (1968) and Roback (1968) agreed that the main—and probably the only—justification for the use of the test is that it can provide a fairly reliable *global* impression of a child's adjustment. However, judgements based on *single* signs in the drawing, such as line quality or the way a particular body part is drawn, are much less reliable. More recently, Kahill (1984), when reviewing the empirical evidence from 1967 to 1982, came to similar conclusions. The value of this test, then, is severely limited; it can act as little more than a rough screening device for determining a child's personality adjustment at a gross level.

Emotional Adjustment

In a similar way that drawings have been used to reveal children's enduring personality traits, they have also been used to assess more temporary emotional adjustment or disturbance. Di Leo (1973), among others, has specified a number of indicators of disturbance in children's figure drawing. These range from the omission of items which normal children would include (torso, arms, mouth, etc.), the inclusion of items such as genitalia which rarely occur in normal children's drawings (in Western cultures, at least), exaggeration or diminution of certain body parts, unconnected or scattered body parts, unusual proportions of the figure, shading and grotesque forms.

The figure drawn by a boy aged 6 years and 10 months (see Fig. 5.2) has no arms, and Di Leo (1973, p. 38) considers that this omission may be a sign of timidity, passivity or intellectual immaturity and, furthermore, an expression of the child's guilt feelings. He also describes the boy as being excessively cautious and non-aggressive. It is true that at this age, most children include the arms in their drawings of the human figure. But some children do not, and without first of all checking to see what the *normal* developmental trends are, it would probably be erroneous to assume that

FIG. 5.2 Omission of arms on a figure drawn by a boy aged 6 years 10 months. (From Di Leo, 1973.)

the omission of a certain body part reflects some emotional problem. Di Leo himself is at pains to emphasise this: "Knowledge of developmental sequences is essential lest one consider deviant what is merely the immaturity of a normally developing psyche" (p. 18).

However, his claim that the omission of the arms indicates timidity and passivity and may also be interpreted as an expression of guilt feelings is questionable. This child may in fact be performing in accordance with his mental age and, if that is lower than his chronological age, this in itself may account for his immature figure. It may have nothing at all to do with his emotional state. Although Di Leo says that his claims are based on a body of expert opinion as well as on his own long experience, we need to have a more concrete, scientific evaluation of these claims before we can accept their validity.

Koppitz's Emotional Indicators

In addition to her 30 developmental items measuring a child's mental maturity (see Chapter 4), Koppitz (1968) lists 30 *emotional indicators* by which a child's emotional adjustment or disturbance may be assessed (see Table 5.1). Many of these indicators were noted by Machover (1949; 1951) and by Di Leo (1973). They include the absence of certain parts of the body (eyes, mouth, legs, feet, neck), a figure height of more than 9 inches or less than 2 inches, a slant of more than 15 degrees from the vertical, very long or very short arms, and the inclusion of extra items such as clouds, rain, snow or flying birds.

Koppitz compared the emotional indicators in the human figure drawings of two groups of children aged between 5 and 12 years. Group 1 comprised 76 children attending ordinary schools and judged by their teachers to be well-adjusted in every way; group 2 comprised 76 children who were patients at a child guidance clinic. Whereas the normal children produced 22 emotional indicators, the clinic children produced 166. Altogether, 58 of the 76 well-adjusted children drew no emotional indicators at all, 14 drew 1 item and 4 children drew 2 items. In contrast, only 7 children in the clinical group drew figures with no emotional indicators and three-quarters of the group drew two or more items. Four items occurred significantly more often at the 0.01 level in the clinical group: poor integration, shading of body and/or limbs, slanting figure and tiny figure. Four more items occurred more often in the clinical group at the 0.05 level of significance: big figure, short arms, cut-off hands and omission of neck.

Koppitz then went on to compare the emotional items in the drawings of different groups of clinical subjects. Children rated as aggressive ($n = 31$) drew more emotional indicators than those rated as shy and withdrawn ($n = 31$): 90 as opposed to 75. The items which were included more often by the aggressive children were asymmetry of limbs ($P<0.05$), teeth ($P<0.05$), long arms ($P<0.01$), big hands ($P<0.05$) and cut-off hands ($P<0.05$); the shy children omitted the mouth more often than did the aggressive children ($P<0.05$). When I re-analysed these data, however, I found that the "big hands" and "no mouth" items did not occur significantly more often in one group than the other.

TABLE 5.1
The 30 Emotional Items in Koppitz's Draw-a-Person Test

1. Poor integration of parts	17. Hands cut off
2. Shading of face	18. Legs pressed together
3. Shading of body and/or limbs	19. Genitals
4. Shading of hands and/or neck	20. Monster or grotesque figure
5. Gross asymmetry of limbs	21. Three or more figures spontaneously
6. Slanting figure	drawn
7. Tiny figure	22. Clouds
8. Big figure	23. No eyes
9. Transparencies	24. No nose
10. Tiny head	25. No mouth
11. Crossed eyes	26. No body
12. Teeth	27. No arms
13. Short arms	28. No legs
14. Long arms	29. No feet
15. Arms clinging to body	30. No neck
16. Big hands	

Koppitz made a further comparison between 35 neurotic children with a history of stealing and 35 children with a history of psychosomatic complaints, such as stomach upsets and headaches. The group with a history of stealing scored more items than the other group: 96 as opposed to 78 items. In this group, there were more figures with big hands ($P<0.05$) and no neck ($P<0.01$); the children with psychosomatic complaints drew more figures with short arms ($P<0.05$). Again, when I re-analysed these data, I found that two items did not occur significantly more often in one group than in the other—big hands and short arms. A further point regarding Koppitz's data analysis concerns the significance levels. As so many chi-squared analyses were carried out, and therefore the risk of making a Type I error would be increased (Clegg, 1982), a more stringent policy would be to accept as significant only those differences with a probability level of 0.01. If we apply this criterion to Koppitz's data, then there are only two items which are significant in the two studies cited above—long arms and no neck.

Despite the fact that some indicators appeared more frequently in some subject groups than in others, Koppitz emphasises that the degree of adjustment or disturbance should be assessed according to a child's *total* number of emotional indicators in the drawing. She gives a clear warning, which echoes the criticisms of Machover made by both Swensen (1968) and Roback (1968), that it is not meaningful to make a diagnosis on the basis of one single indicator because problems and anxieties may be expressed in different ways by different children and in different ways by the same child on different occasions. It is nonsense, then, to say, "This figure has no arms, therefore the child must be anxious or disturbed". Furthermore, Koppitz (1968, p. 55) urges us to consider not only the *total* number of indicators but to analyse them on the basis of the child's age and social and cultural background and, in addition, to evaluate them together with other available data.

Experimental Interest

In recent years, experimental psychologists have turned their attention to some of the claims made by clinicians about children's human figure drawings. Their approach has been to consider what they would think of as a more parsimonious explanation for the phenomena under consideration. In general, their hypotheses concern issues to do with the planning and arrangement of, for example, the different body parts of a single figure or the organisation of a group of figures on the page. These hypotheses are primarily concerned with production strategies and have been tested on the whole with normal children rather than with clinical samples. I shall review work carried out on three main issues: disproportionately sized heads, figure size and distance between figures.

Large Heads

One claim that routinely appears in the literature is that children exaggerate the size of a body part which is important or has particular significance for them. In particular, it is the head of the young child's figure which appears to be so large. The reason for this, as Di Leo (1973) argues, is that to a child the head is the most important part of a person and, indeed, the most symbolic; at the tadpole stage, the head completely dominates the figure, but even when the child introduces the torso, the primacy of the head is still proclaimed by its exaggerated size.

In Chapter 3, I suggested that there might be other reasons for the disproportionately large heads on the figures drawn by most children below the age of about 8 years (Nash & Harris, 1970; Schuyten, 1904): first, the head gets more than its fair share of space because it is normally drawn first and, secondly, the outline of the head is drawn large in order to accommodate the facial features. The results of more recent studies (e.g. Henderson & Thomas, 1990; Selfe, 1983; Thomas & Tsalimi, 1988) show that head and torso size is certainly affected by the process of planning that is involved in the child's drawing of the human figure. For example, if children are asked to draw the torso first and then the head or to draw a head onto a pre-drawn torso, they exaggerate the head size much less. Further, if they are asked to include details on the *torso* of the figure they will make the outline of the torso bigger, but if they are asked to draw the back view of a person (which has few detailed features) the exaggeration of the head size is much less.

Important People are Taller

In parallel with the art of the Ancient Egyptians, in which royal figures are taller than civilians and civilians are taller than slaves, it has been suggested that the exaggerated size of some figures in children's drawings indicates their special significance and the diminished size of others reflects their insignificance (Löwenfeld, 1939; Löwenfeld & Brittain, 1975, p. 188). These differences in size may be significant but are not necessarily conscious (Gellert, 1968).

The claim regarding the exaggerated size of important figures was investigated in three studies (Craddick, 1961; Sechrest & Wallace, 1964; Solley & Haigh, 1957), which made the assumption that Santa Claus increases in importance for North American children as Christmas approaches. Although it was found that the figures increased in size nearer to Christmas and then decreased again afterwards, there were various problems. One problem is that no account was taken of the fact that children become more familiar with pictures of Santa Claus towards Christmas and might draw their own figure larger in order to include the details they have become aware of. In fact, Wallach and Leggett (1972) found that in their sample, the size of Santa Claus did not decrease after Christmas, a finding which is more in accord with this familiarisation view and against the "decrease in importance" idea.

Another hypothesis regarding the supposed link between the sizes of figures in a drawing and their importance in the child's life is that the size differences may actually be more to do with planning problems in the organisation of a group of figures on the page. The same kinds of issues apply as in the case in which the size of the head is drawn disproportion-ately large in comparison with the torso (see Chapter 3). Similarly, the order in which each figure is drawn and the space available may be important considerations. The first figure may be at an advantage in that there are fewer constraints on space and subsequent figures may be smaller because there is less space left on the page.

Fox and Thomas (n.d.) investigated the size of figures in the drawings of 4- to 9-year-olds. They removed the problem of the available space on the page by asking the children to draw each figure on a separate sheet. They first asked the children to draw a picture of their mother and one of an ordinary woman; half the children drew their mother first and half drew the ordinary woman first. On another occasion, they were asked to draw their father and an ordinary man. Most of the children made larger drawings of their parents than they did of the ordinary people, whether the pictures of their parents were drawn first or second.

Threatening People are Smaller

Craddick (1963) claimed that drawers reduce the size of threatening or anxiety-evoking figures; for example, Hallowe'en witches were smaller during Hallowe'en than those drawn before or after. Fox and Thomas (1990) compared children's drawings of Hallowe'en witches and those of ordinary women 1 week before, 1 day before and 1 week after Hallowe'en. They also used a questionnaire to assess the children's fear of witches. In their first study, they found that the drawings of witches and women were significantly smaller at Hallowe'en rather than 1 week before; both figures were larger after Hallowe'en than at Hallowe'en, although the difference was not significant. In general, then, there seemed little support for Craddick's hypothesis. However, Fox and Thomas spotted a potential problem with this conclusion: How do we know that the children actually had a fear of witches? If they did not, then there would be no need for them to reduce their size.

In their second study, Fox and Thomas compared the drawings of those children who were afraid of witches with those who were not. Those who were scared drew their witches smaller and their ordinary women larger compared with the drawings of the children who weren't scared. This finding does support the view that children may try to diminish the extent of their fear by reducing the size of a threatening topic.

Nice and Nasty

One problem that Thomas identified regarding the children's drawings of their parents compared with those of ordinary people was that the parent figures might be drawn larger because the children were intending to include more details in their outlines, irrespective of whether they regard their parents as important figures. Thomas, Chaigne, and Fox (1989) asked 4- to 7-year-olds to copy only the outline of a figure so that they did not have to consider the amount of space that would be needed for any extra features. They were then asked to copy the figure again, but this time they had to imagine the figure to be *either* a very nice person "who is kind and caring" *or* a very nasty person "who steals sweets and things". Those children who drew a nice person drew their figures larger and those who drew a nasty person drew them smaller than their "neutral" figures; another group of children, who drew the neutral figure twice, did not vary the size of their drawings significantly. This size effect occurred again when children were asked to draw a nice or a nasty magic apple, showing that the effect is not confined to animate objects. So, again, we have evidence that important or nice people/things are drawn larger than nasty people/ things.

Although these studies are useful, they are nevertheless somewhat artificial, since children usually draw groups of figures on the same page. If the order of drawing the figures and/or their position on the page can be controlled, do they still draw nice people larger and nasty figures smaller? A further study by Cotterill and Thomas (1990) has revealed, rather suprisingly, that the size effect is actually reversed if the child is asked to draw two figures or compare two figures on the same page: the nasty figure is now the larger one and the nice figure is the smaller one. Clearly, this result is in direct contrast not only to Thomas's earlier studies, but also to the common claim about the relative size difference between nice and nasty figures. As yet, however, this recent finding has not been replicated, so it is really too early to accept its reliability.

Distance Between Figures

A notion widely held in clinical practice (e.g. Di Leo, 1973; Koppitz, 1968; Machover, 1949; 1951) is that the distance between the child's drawing of herself and other figures in the scene indicates something about the child's emotional attitude towards those figures. In particular, closer proximity on the page also reflects closer emotional affinity in reality. In order to test this assumption, Thomas and Gray (1992) asked 36 4- to 5-year-olds and 36 5- to 6-year-olds to finish off two pre-drawn figures representing themselves which had been started on two separate sheets of paper. Within each age group, the children were allocated to two different conditions. In the *separate sheets* condition, they were asked to add a "best friend" on one sheet and a "child you don't like very much" on the other (to the left of the self in each case). In the *same sheet* condition, a self-figure was centrally placed on a single sheet of paper and the children were asked to draw the best friend and the third figure to the left and to the right of the self-figure. In both conditions, half the children drew the friend first and half drew the non-friend first.

Thomas and Gray measured the distance between the centre of the head of the pre-drawn figure and the tip of the nose of the added figure. Both liked and disliked figures were drawn farther away from the self in the separate sheets condition than in the same sheet condition. In the separate sheets condition, the disliked figure was drawn significantly farther from the self-figure than was the liked figure, thus supporting the hypothesis. There was no significant difference in the same sheet condition, however; in fact, there was a non-significant tendency for the disliked person to be drawn nearer to, and the liked person to be drawn more distant from, the self.

These findings seem to fit in with Thomas's previous findings for the drawings of nice and nasty people, where the size effect was reversed when the two figures were on the same page or on separate pages. This effect could be to do with the spatial/order problems of drawing more than one figure on the same sheet. In the separate sheets condition, the child has only one reference figure, which is positioned to the left-hand side, and draws the added figure to the right in each case. This is not true for the same sheet condition: For one figure the child draws to the left and for the other to the right of the reference figure; furthermore, the second added figure obviously has to be positioned in relation to the two figures already there.

Summary

As well as being used as guides to children's levels of intellectual functioning, human figure drawings have also been used to assess their personality and emotional adjustment. The claims made about specific features of a child's drawing, however, have been based largely on intuition and individual practitioners' experience. When researchers have attempted to verify the claims, they have in the main failed to reach agreement; this having been said, however, many of the research studies themselves were poorly controlled. At least one can conclude that it is not valid at the present time to impute particular problems to a child on the basis of very specific features in her drawing, features such as the height of the figure, the omission of a mouth, long arms, etc.

What does seem a reasonable use of children's human figure drawings is as a more general indicator of a child's problems, since on Koppitz's list of 30 emotional items, children who were referred for clinical treatment produced more of these than did normal children. Thus, the items indicate a problem in a quantitative way but cannot be relied upon in themselves to help specify the exact nature of a child's difficulties.

More recent experimental research with children in the normal range has investigated the reasons for some of the notable characteristics of children's drawings, characteristics such as disproportionately large heads and marked differences in size between figures known in reality to be fairly similar. The findings of these studies indicate that explanations in terms of the child's planning of the drawing and the spatial arrangement of the figures on the page may well account, at least in part, for some of the classic characteristics. Thus, before making assumptions about the meaning of a child's drawing in terms of her personality and/or emotional adjustment, researchers and practitioners should be sure that the so-called emotional indicators in the drawing are not merely a result of difficulties in planning. Of course, it is recognised that the two kinds of explanation are not necessarily mutually exclusive: It may be that emotional disturbance in a child is related to difficulties in planning, both in drawing and also in other tasks.

6

Sex Differences in Children's Human Figure Drawings

Topics Selected in Spontaneous Drawings

In Western cultures, as Lark-Horovitz et al. (1973) point out, males are typically interested in machines, transportation, and the like, and this interest is reflected in their drawings; boys are also interested in portraying movement and figures in action. The characteristics of girls' pictures, in contrast, tend to be of static scenes with much detail and decoration; their human figures are more detailed than those of boys (Goodenough, 1926; Harris, 1963; Knopf & Richards, 1952). This difference in topic choice may explain why boys have been noted to alter the rigid schema of the human figure at an earlier age than girls (Goodenough, 1926) and also experiment earlier with perspective representations, leading Kerschensteiner (1905), for example, to report that boys excel in nearly all kinds of drawing, except in "certain kinds of decorative design". It should also be noted, however, that boys in Munich at that time, and indeed boys in London, were allowed more time in the curriculum for drawing and therefore had more instruction and more practice in drawing, and for this reason alone it is perhaps not surprising that Cyril Burt (1921) declared that boys were "eminently superior to the girls".

This association between the sex of the artist and the particular choice of subject matter is not necessarily universal and may be conditioned by the prevailing culture. On the island of Alor in the former East Indies (Du Bois, 1944), for example, girls drew tools four times more frequently than did boys, while boys drew decorative and detailed pictures of human figures, spirits and flowers far more than did girls, a finding which contradicts the usual Western stereotype of sex-related topics.

91

That Western children do hold very strong stereotypes about what might be a typical activity for males and females is evident in a study by Papadakis-Michaelides (1989), who asked 240 children aged between 4 years 6 months and 10 years 6 months to draw a man and a lady "doing something". The most common activity chosen for the female figures was housework and that for the males was sport, and this was equally true in the drawings produced by boys and girls (see Table 6.1).

Are Boys Ahead of Girls?

Even though various researchers in the early part of the twentieth century commented on the superiority of boys' ability to draw, girls are actually in advance of boys in terms of the number of details included in their human figures (see Chapter 4). Both Goodenough (1926) and Harris (1963) noted the advantage in this respect that girls have over boys at all ages except 12 and gave separate norms in their scoring system. Similar findings have been reported by Knopf and Richards (1952), Richards and Ross (1967), O'Keefe et al. (1971), Laosa, Swartz, and Holtzman (1973) and Ford, Stern, and Dillon (1974). In general, girls draw their figures taller than do boys (Papadakis-Michaelides, 1989) and one reason may be that they do this in anticipation of the greater amount of detail they intend to include in their figures.

Although girls are in advance of boys as regards the detail of their human figure drawings, it might be more in keeping with the spirit of the earlier claims, by Kerschensteiner (1905) and Burt (1921) for example, about boys' superiority if we look at evidence regarding the *way* the figures are drawn rather than the amount of detail they contain. We might seek evidence on the following three aspects of drawing: the way the limbs of the figure are depicted, the frequency of contouring and the frequency of profiling.

It is acknowledged that the use of double lines to denote arms and legs is developmentally more advanced than the use of single lines (see Chapter 3). Willsdon (1977) found that, in his sample of 634 boys and 608 girls

TABLE 6.1
Percentage of Boys and Girls Drawing Their Male and Female Figures Engaged in Housework and Sport

| | Boys | | Girls | |
	Males	Females	Males	Females
Housework	6.6	35.8	5.8	28.3
Sport	31.0	8.3	26.6	8.3

between the ages of 4 years 6 months and 7 years 6 months, girls introduced double lines for legs 6 months ahead of the boys and they introduced double lines for arms 12 months ahead of the boys.

I examined the segmented conventional figure drawings of 86 boys and 86 girls between the ages of 3 years and 7 years 6 months in order to check Willsdon's findings. There was no difference in age between the 24 boys and the 36 girls who used single lines for the arms: the mean age of both groups was 5 years 1 month (with a standard deviation of 10 and 11 months, respectively). Similarly, there was no significant age difference between the 36 boys and 47 girls in their use of single lines for the legs: boys averaged 4 years 11 months (SD 13 months) and girls averaged 5 years (SD 10 months). There was a difference, however, in the use of double lines for the limbs: the average age for girls was 5 years 7 months, whereas the average for boys was 5 years 11 months. Altogether, 41 girls and 52 boys had used double lines for the arms and 38 girls and 48 boys had used them for the legs. Although the four months difference is not as dramatic as the difference found by Willsdon, nevertheless it confirms his findings and also refutes the claims made by some earlier authors. Not only is there no evidence in favour of boys, but in fact the difference is in the other direction, in favour of girls.

Let us turn to the evidence relating to the contouring and profiling of figures, bearing in mind Goodenough's (1926) observation that boys alter their rigid schemas of the human figure at an earlier age than do girls. When I examined the human figure drawings of 118 5- to 6-year-olds, 127 7- to 8-year-olds and 99 9- to 10-year-olds (see Chapter 3), I actually found no significant sex differences in the amount of contouring (see Table 6.2) or the amount of profiling (see Table 6.3) either in their standard drawings of the human figure or in their running figures.

TABLE 6.2

Frequency of Contouring in the Standard and Running Figures Drawn by Boys and Girls in Three Age Groups (Percentages in Parentheses)

| | *Age Groups* | | |
	5–6 years	*7–8 years*	*9–10 years*
Standard	n = 118	n = 127	n = 99
Boys	17 (30)	54 (81)	46 (94)
Girls	14 (23)	49 (82)	49 (98)
Running	n = 112	n = 115	n = 118
Boys	13 (23)	40 (70)	58 (91)
Girls	14 (25)	46 (79)	50 (93)

TABLE 6.3

Frequency of Profiling in the Standard and Running Figures Drawn by Boys and Girls in Three Age Groups (Percentages in Parentheses)

	Age Groups		
	5–6 years	*7–8 years*	*9–10 years*
Standard	*n* = 118	*n* = 127	*n* = 99
Boys	7 (12)	13 (19)	8 (16)
Girls	9 (15)	7 (12)	13 (26)
Running	*n* = 112	*n* = 115	*n* = 118
Boys	25 (45)	41 (72)	56 (88)
Girls	22 (39)	40 (69)	43 (80)

Sexual Preference

Many studies have found that most children prefer to draw their own sex first in a free drawing task (see Table 6.4). It is often assumed that the sex of the figure drawn first by the artist in a free drawing task reflects his or her sex role identification, role preference or sexual orientation (see Chapter 5). Granick and Smith (1953), however, doubted this explanation, since they could find no correlation between figure preference and attitudinal masculinity or femininity orientation, as measured by the Minnesota Multiphasic Personality Inventory, devised by Hathaway and McKinley (1940). In an extensive review of the literature, Brown and Tolor (1957) also doubted the notion that the choice of sex in figure drawing reflects the drawer's psychosexual identification or adjustment. And, having reviewed 19 studies, Heinrich and Triebe (1972) concluded that children's preference for drawing their own sex first was probably due to cultural factors rather than to personality development.

TABLE 6.4

Percentages of Boys and Girls Drawing Their Own Sex First

Study	n	Age Range (Years)	% Boys	% Girls
Weider and Noller (1950)	153	8–10	74	97
Weider and Noller (1953)	438	7–12	70	94
Knopf and Richards (1952)	20	6	80	50
Knopf and Richards (1952)	20	8	80	70
Jolles (1952)	2560	5–12	85	80
Tolor and Tolor (1955)	136	9–12	82	91
Tolor and Tolor (1974)	132	10–12	91	94
Papadakis-Michaelides (1989)	507	3;6–11;5	73.4	78.6

Differentiation of Male and Female Figures by Boys and Girls

Below the age of about 5 years, there is virtually no attempt to denote the sex of a figure (Mott, 1954); at kindergarten, however, children begin to use sexually differentiating features (Mott, 1954) and the use of these increases with age (Papadakis-Michaelides, 1989). Sexually differentiating items have been found to be used earlier by girls than by boys (Papadakis-Michaelides, 1989; Willsdon, 1977) and female figures are drawn with more sexually differentiating items than are the male figures (Papadakis-Michaelides, 1989). Of course, it may be that in Western cultures there actually *are* more gender-specific items for females, e.g. various items of jewellery, handbags, etc.

Swensen (1955) and Swensen and Newton (1955) devised a 9-point scale for adequacy of sexual differentiation between figures. They found that, up to about the age of 12 years, girls exceeded boys, but that there was no difference among the older boys and girls. Murphy (1957), however, found that among adults, women scored higher than men on the adequacy of differentiation of the two figures.

The feature that very young children mainly use to differentiate their figures is hairstyle or hair length: curly hair (Mott, 1954) or long hair (Arazos & Davis, 1989; Di Leo, 1970; Sitton & Light, 1992) is used for females and bald heads or short hair for males (Arazos & Davis, 1989; Sitton & Light, 1992; see Fig. 6.1). These studies have also noted the triangular torsos given to females and the increasing use of clothes to differentiate the sexes.

A further differentiating feature is the height of the figure. Since men are on average taller than women, one might expect this difference in height to be reflected in children's drawings and, indeed, Ford (1977) found that in his sample of 166 children's human figure drawings, the average height of male figures was greater than the height of female figures. Although Sitton and Light (1992) found no difference between the height of male and female figures, both Arazos and Davis (1989) and Bradbury and Papadakis-Michaelides (1990) have found that both boys and, to a greater extent girls, draw their female figures taller than their male figures; the difference in height is not related to the order in which the figures are drawn.

Although the size of the figure may be related to the amount of detail included in it, Arazos and Davis (1989) explain their results in terms of other production factors, i.e. that the long hair of female figures may lead the children to increase the body length and the long skirt may also lead to an increase in the leg length. Thus, there is some confounding of the variables which are used to indicate the sex of a figure.

FIG. 6.1   The gender cues used to distinguish male and female figures are hair and, later, clothing. Drawings of (a) a man, (b) a woman, (c) a boy and (d) a girl by 4-year-olds (top), 5-year-olds (centre) and 6-year-olds (bottom). (Reprinted with the permission of the *British Journal of Developmental Psychology* and **Professor Paul Light.**)

Arazos and Davis (1989) tried to disentangle these variables and to find out which were more important. First, they presented pairs of pictures to their 4- to 7-year-olds and asked them to say which was the girl and which was the boy (see Fig. 6.2). They found that figures with short hair, figures with trousers and taller figures were all designated boys. They then set about putting these features into conflict by presenting such pairs as a short-haired figure in a skirt and a long-haired figure in trousers. The results showed that the overriding cue for gender was the length of the

FIG. 6.2 Eight pairs of figures used in a study by Arazos and Davis (1989). In each pair, the percentage of children identifying a particular figure as the boy or the girl is shown. (Reproduced with the permission of Dr Alyson Davis.)

hair, followed by the type of clothes (skirt or trousers), and last of all the relative heights of the figures.

In a further task, the children were given two pre-drawn heads or two pre-drawn torsos and were asked to complete the figures. Given the pre-drawn torsos, the children generally used hair length to discriminate their two figures. Given the two pre-drawn heads, however, the children did not use markedly different torso shapes in their completion of the figures. Again, it seems that hair length is the most important feature for marking the gender of the figures.

Explicit Sexual Features

In Western cultures, it is unusual to see explicit genitalia on children's drawings of the human figure (Ames & Ilg, 1963; Di Leo, 1973; Koppitz, 1968; Rosen & Boe, 1968), except in graffiti drawings intended to be shocking and/or obscene. The presence of genitalia on children's human figure drawings may alarm parents and professionals, particularly in the light of the increasing number of reported cases of sexual abuse of children. Although rape victims will often draw genitalia on their figures when, during therapy, they are asked to depict their experiences (Burgess, McCausland, & Wolbert, 1981; Kelley, 1985), no satisfactory study has been carried out which has compared the incidence of genitalia in the standard figure drawings of these children compared with suitable control groups. The few studies which have been reported have had severe limitations, such as small samples, drawings collected in uncontrolled conditions, and subjective or unsystematic analyses (Burgess et al., 1981; Goodwin, 1982; Kelley, 1985; Wohl & Kaufman, 1985; Yates, Beutler, & Crago, 1985). Thus, although the inclusion of genitalia in the child's drawing may indicate sexual maladjustment or overconcern with the genitals brought about by sexual abuse or by a recent operation such as herniorrhaphy or circumcision (Di Leo, 1970), there is no reliable evidence for any of these conclusions.

The rarity of genitalia in normal children's drawings may not be universal, however. Fortes (1940), for example, reported that among the Tallensi, an African culture with no representational art, children typically drew pin-head figures in which the facial features were omitted but the sexual parts were accentuated. In societies such as these, it may be that people's sexual parts are normally more visible to children who then use these as defining or differentiating features in their drawings; in Western societies, in contrast, sexual parts are normally less obvious, so that children are perhaps more likely to use other features such as hairstyle and clothing to denote the sex of their figures. Another explanation is one of taboo. In Western societies, explicit depiction of the genitalia is rare and is generally regarded as inappropriate (exceptions are medical and educational texts, some examples of fine art and pornographic material). It may be that in some other societies, the Talle for example, this taboo does not operate. Indeed, since there was no tradition at all of representing the human form among the Tallensi, it might reasonably be assumed that when the children were asked to draw they felt no inhibition about depicting the genitalia.

Summary

Despite early claims that boys' drawing is more advanced than girls', there is actually little support for this view. In fact, in some respects, for example the amount of detail in a figure and the way the limbs are drawn, girls are in advance of boys. As well as these differences, there are also differences in children's preference for the figure they draw first: boys draw males first, whereas girls draw females. Female figures are usually drawn with more sexually differentiating items than are male figures, and girls add more of these than do boys. The earliest feature used to differentiate the figures is hair length—bald heads or short hair for male figures and long hair for females. Increasingly with age, both boys and girls differentiate their figures with gender-appropriate clothing and other adornments. In general in Western societies, explicit genitalia are not included in children's figure drawings, perhaps because they are simply not visible when the figure is clothed but also because the display and depiction of genitalia is not normally regarded as appropriate.

7 Human Figure Drawings in Different Cultures

The Importance of the Human Figure

The fact that whole books and papers have been written about children's human figure drawings and that diagnostic tests have been developed based solely on them (see Chapters 4 and 5), suggests that the human figure itself is especially important. It certainly does appear to be one of the earliest topics that children draw and remains popular throughout childhood (see Introduction). And a number of researchers have no doubts about its significance: "We have chosen to have children draw men, rather than food or plants because their choices of men have greater social significance" (Dennis, 1966, p. 5) and "Because the human being is so basically important to him [the child], affectively as well as cognitively, it is probable that the human figure is a better index [for concept development] than, for example, a house or an automobile" (Harris, 1963, p. 7). Based on the assumption of its universal importance, Di Leo (1970, p. 224) claimed that, as a consequence, "The Goodenough Draw-a-Man Test is probably as close as we have come to the ideal of a culture-free test of intelligence."

Artistic Cultures

At the beginning of the twentieth century, when the study of anthropology was beginning to flourish, a number of authors published papers on the drawings made by children and adults in different cultures, in British New Guinea (Haddon, 1904), the Belgian Congo (Dégallier, 1905) and Algeria

(Probst, 1906), for example. In 1932, Paget published his findings based on over 60,000 children's drawings of the human figure collected from all over the world.

Using scoring systems such as that devised by Goodenough (1926) and Harris (1963), many researchers reported differences in the human figure drawings among a range of different cultural groups. Havighurst, Gunther, and Pratt (1946), for example, compared 6- to 11-year-old American-Indian children in six different tribes and found that these children had higher scores than white children. They noted that in these Indian groups, art had a high status among the adults and the Indian children practised drawing more than did white children.

Whereas profile figures do not appear in Western children's standard human figure drawings until about the age of 9 years (see Chapter 3) and are generally regarded as a more advanced form, Paget (1932) found that among 4000 drawings produced by 967 Maori children in New Zealand, the proportion of profile figures rose from 61% at age 5 years to 88% at age 8 years (see Fig. 7.1). Fortes (1981) has also remarked on the profile orientation of the figures drawn by Tallensi children attending a boarding school in the 1930s and those attending the local primary school in 1970.

In modern China, the graphic arts are held in high esteem and children are given formal tuition in calligraphy, drawing and painting, beginning in the kindergarten (see Winner, 1989). Although there has been no comparative study of their human figure drawings, there is some evidence

FIG. 7.1   Man in profile, drawn by a Maori boy aged 5 years. (From Paget, 1932.)

that Chinese children's drawing skills in general are considerably more advanced than those of children in the West (Cox, 1992; Winner, 1989).

Non-representational Art

There are some cultures which, in contrast, have no established tradition of representational art and one would therefore predict that children's— and indeed adults'—attempts at drawing the human figure would score rather low on diagnostic tests. For example, among the Bedouin, drawing is rarely practised and, consequently, their children's drawings, which Dennis (1960) found to be very basic and poor in detail, received very low scores.

A study carried out in Turkey by Cox and Bayraktar (1989) also provides evidence for the relatively poor performance of both children and illiterate adults living in areas in which drawing is rarely practised and indeed pictures are infrequently seen (see Table 7.1). Rather than assessing the figure drawings according to one of the standardised scoring systems, we classified their structure into the five categories originally used by Cox and Parkin (1986): scribbles, distinct shapes, tadpoles, transitional figures and conventional figures. Whereas Turkish urban adults and children draw conventional figures, the majority of the children and half the adults tested in a rural area drew much less mature figures (see Fig. 7.2). Bayraktar has recently collected drawings from a further group of urban, illiterate adults who originated from the countryside and had been living in Ankara for between 10 and 15 years. Since these adults would have been more exposed to pictures in the city than in the country, one would expect more of them to draw conventional figures, and indeed this was the case, although nearly a third of them still drew less mature figures.

TABLE 7.1
Classification of Figure Drawings Completed by Turkish and UK Children and Adults

Subjects and Age Range (Years)	Scribbles	Distinct Shapes	Tadpoles	Transitionals	Conventionals
Turkish adults					
Urban (17–23)					30
Rural (16–27)			7	8	15
Rural/urban (21–65)	1		16	6	45
Turkish children					
Urban (3;7–5;5)			5	3	22
Rural (3–6)	3		13	6	8
UK					
Adults (18;0–22;2)					30
Children (3;8–5;8)			3	2	25

Girl aged 3 years

Boy aged 6 years

Boy aged 5 years

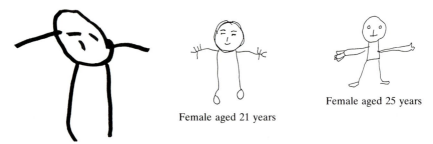

Female aged 23 years

Female aged 21 years

Female aged 25 years

FIG. 7.2   Figures produced by Turkish children (top) and adults (bottom) in a rural area. (Reproduced with the permission of Professor Rüvide Bayraktar.)

Changing Traditions

It is well-known that in Eskimo societies there is a long tradition of carving in, for example, bone, ivory and soapstone (Canadian Eskimo Arts Council, 1971), and Harris (1963) found a superior drawing ability among the 318 Eskimo children he tested in several remote Alaskan schools. Recently, one of my students, Aileen Hope, who grew up with the Inuit in Canada and was herself fluent in Inuktitut, investigated the drawing and modelling abilities of 45 children in three age groups (6–7, 9–10 and 14–15 years) living on Southampton Island in the North West Territories of Canada. Using the Goodenough–Harris scoring system (Harris, 1963), she compared their performance with that of 40 Scottish children in the same age ranges. To our surprise, the Inuit children scored significantly *lower* in both drawing and clay-modelling than did the Scottish children at all age levels. Despite this difference in scores, there was actually little difference between the Inuit and Scottish drawings in the structure of the figures, particularly in the youngest and the oldest groups: In both societies, most of the youngest children drew segmented conventional figures and most of the eldest drew figures which showed some degree of contouring. At age 9–10, however, whereas 60% of the Inuit children showed contouring, all of the Scottish children did so.

When we compare the Inuit and Scottish groups on their modelled figures, although there was no apparent difference in the frequency of use of the modelling tools, there were nevertheless some differences in both the final structure of the models and the way the clay was used. For example, whereas no Scottish 6- to 7-year-old produced a tadpole form, 73% of the Inuit did so. Furthermore, the youngest Scottish children tended to break off clay pieces which they then moulded and reattached as arms and legs, etc.; the Inuit, in contrast, tended to leave the clay in one cylindrical block and then incise features into it with a modelling tool (see Fig. 7.3), a technique similar to that used for carving bone or stone.

Of course, Hope's samples are much smaller than Harris's (1963) and it could be that they were simply not representative of the cultures being compared. There are apparently other communities, in Cape Dorset for example (Brundege & Fisher, 1990), which have a greater reputation for excellence in the graphic arts than the one Hope used. Nevertheless, she prefers to explain the relatively poor performance of her Inuit sample in terms of a general shift in emphasis away from traditional artistic skills. Although resources are reasonably good in their schools, there is a distinct

FIG. 7.3   An Inuit boy's model of a person. (Reproduced with the permission of Aileen Hope.)

lack of drawing materials in Inuit homes compared with Scottish homes and the handing down of artistic skills from the old to the young seems to be waning as the old, traditional ways in general disappear.

Minority Groups

There is some evidence that lower-status groups which do not have a particular artistic tradition score low in their drawing performance compared with children of the wider culture. Hilger, Klett, and Watson (1976), for example, found that among Japanese 6-year-olds, a minority group called the Ainu had lower scores than did other children. Interestingly, although these authors had also found that the Japanese scored higher than Americans, when Adler (1971) scored the drawings of Japanese children living in America he found that they scored lower than the American children. He concluded that these cultural differences in scores most probably reflected the relative social status of a group within a wider culture rather than genetic factors.

In some minority cultural groups, however, such as immigrant Indian and Pakistani families in the UK, parents expect high performance in their children's school work and this general expectation of high achievement may explain why Sinha (1971) found that these children also scored higher than whites on their drawings of the opposite sex (although not on their same-sex drawings). In Moslem societies, although there is a strong tradition of abstract, decorative art, representational art is perhaps relatively less important, and if one were to make predictions on this basis alone one would expect Moslem children to perform relatively low on human figure drawing tasks.

The Importance of the Human Figure is Relative

These kinds of comparisons among different cultural groups are in fact deeply problematic, since the human figure may not have the same special significance in all cultures. In a study of children's drawings on the island of Alor in the former East Indies, Du Bois (1944) found that human figures appeared in only 7% of the 33 boys' drawings and 1% of the 22 girls' drawings. Plants, animals and buildings accounted for 64% of the boys' figures; plants, tools and buildings made up 84% of the girls' figures.

Court (1989) is also extremely critical of the assumption that the human figure is equally common in the drawings of all cultures and that one can use it as a culture-free measure of comparison. In her studies of children in Kenya, she found that when given a free choice of subject-matter, rural Kikuyu children drew houses more frequently than they drew people. Similarly, only about a quarter of a group of Luo 11- to 18-years-olds

($n = 21$) and Samburu 10- to 18-year-olds ($n = 24$) drew people; when they did draw them, their figures were small with little detail and, rather than standing alone, they accompanied other more significant imagery such as boats (for the Luo) and animals (for the Samburu). Although in contrast, 76% of the Kamba ($n = 25$, age 10–15 years) drew human figures, they did not emphasise the expression or detail of individuals but preferred to portray them in active ways and in social contexts.

Even when these different groups were asked to draw "myself eating", they depicted a *social* situation rather than an individual event: 83% of the Samburu, 87% of the Kikuyu and 96% of the Kamba and Luo children drew themselves with other people. As well as the children's interpretation of the topic in this social way, Court also noted the dominance of the table in the scenes. All of the Kamba and Luo children and over 50% of the Samburu drew a table, despite the fact that Court has never seen a table in a Samburu dwelling. She speculates that the presence of the table might reflect the children's aspirations for modernity and an improved standard of living. These examples indicate that there are some cultures in which the individual human figure is not the main focus of attention in children's drawings.

The Graphic Symbol for a Person

Whether or not the human figure *per se* is of great significance, its depiction in some cultural groups is usually very basic, sometimes consisting of what Court calls "global schemata". As she observes, very many children seem to have little concern for making a visual likeness of a person. This difference in intention regarding the appropriate representation of a person is exemplified even more clearly in the drawings of the Walbiri, an Aboriginal group in Australia studied by Munn (1973; Wales, 1990). In this culture, women make symbols in the sand to illustrate their dreaming-stories and Munn reckons there are 16 or more of these symbols. Although some of the symbols, such as a wavy line which can be used for a snake, a river or dancers, seem to echo the visual and movement properties of their referents, others, such as a semi-circle used to represent a person, seem to be much more arbitrary.

Despite the fact that they have real people around them all the time who could serve as models, Walbiri children do not attempt to draw a visual "look-a-like" of a person; rather, they adopt the semi-circle symbol used by the adult women in their sand-drawings. It is only with schooling and exposure to Western styles that the children begin to mix the different representations in their drawings. Thus, the nature of adult art in a culture may determine not only whether children produce any drawings at all which are representational (Fortes, 1940; 1981), but also the particular way that certain objects are actually represented.

Problems for Cross-cultural Research

When comparing drawings in different cultures, then, there are a number of problems. One is that drawing, and indeed other art forms, may or may not normally be practised in a particular culture and may or may not be regarded as a high-status activity. Secondly, topics which seem to be of particular importance in one culture do not necessarily have the same importance in another. Thirdly, different cultural groups may choose to represent a particular topic, such as the human figure, in very different ways.

One of the essential questions in cross-cultural research, as Court (1989, p. 68) points out, is "Does drawing mean the same thing to the various groups under investigation?" From the examples given above, it seems that it does not. And one of the main implications is that we cannot make evaluations of children's human figure drawings in different cultures using criteria—such as those which underpin the Draw-a-Man test—developed in one culture but not necessarily appropriate in another. In other words, these tests cannot be universally valid. This does not mean that cross-cultural comparisons are not a legitimate area of study. On the contrary, they are both interesting and important. But the sensible question to ask is not "Do some cultural groups perform better or worse than others?", but "How and why do cultures differ in the way they depict (or, in some cases, do not depict) the human form?"

Cultural Variations in Human Figure Drawings

I have already mentioned that in some cultures (e.g. the Walbiri) there appears to be no attempt to represent the visual likeness of a person: the semi-circle is so arbitrary that it stands in relation to its referent in almost the same way that the letter "I" in English refers to oneself. In most cultural groups, however, we do at least recognise some visual equivalence between the drawing and a real person, even though compared with Western figures, some supposedly essential body parts may have been omitted and other more peripheral ones have been included and exaggerated, the way that certain body parts are drawn may be very different, and the figure overall may have been put together in a different way.

One striking omission to Western eyes is the omission of facial features in many African drawings. Fortes (1940; 1981), for example, studied the Tallensi in the Northern Territories of the Gold Coast (now Ghana), a society which had no tradition of two-dimensional representational art. Interestingly, the children already had experience of modelling 3- to 4-inch high clay figures and they poked depressions into the head in order to represent the eyes, nose and mouth. Yet, when a group of 6- to

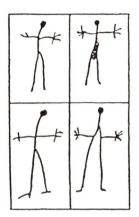

FIG. 7.4   Pin-head figures drawn by Bemba children (Rhodesia). (From Paget, 1932.)

16-year-olds first used pencil and paper, they drew their human figures as stick figures with "pin"-heads, omitting the facial features. Paget (1932) also illustrated some examples of pin-head figures among the Bemba tribe in Rhodesia in his report of children's human figure drawings (see Fig. 7.4).

Similarly, when Reuning and Wortley (1973) asked Kalahari Bushmen to draw the human figure, they also produced pin-head figures. However, it should be noted that they drew their pictures in the sand and the use of this medium may have precluded the drawing of facial details. Although the researchers also asked their subjects to make pencil and paper drawings, they explain that this was an informal and exploratory session and they do not give any details of the drawings which were produced. We do not know, then, whether or not the Bushmen repeated the pin-head style or whether they drew in the facial features.

A feature which is often included in the drawings from other cultural groups but omitted in Western figures is the genitalia. Whereas Di Leo (1973) had seen only six cases among thousands in which the penis or vulva had been clearly portayed, Fortes (1940) mentioned the accentuation of the sexual features among the drawings made by the Talle subjects he studied. Explanations for these differences have already been outlined in Chapter 6.

A Difference in Structure

A difference in the overall structure of the figure has been noted by several researchers. Whereas Children in Western cultures tend to encompass each major body part of the figure, such as the head and the torso, with its own contour and then place the facial features or the torso features within each of these regions, children in some other cultures prefer chain-type drawings in which each feature, from head to toe, is added to the vertical line of the figure. The figure seems to have been constructed in a list-like way, starting with a region for the head, followed by eyes placed symmetrically around the vertical axis, followed by the nostrils placed in a similar way, then the mouth, the chin, the neck, and so on. Paget (1932) noticed these chain figures (see Fig. 7.5), drawn by children in Africa and in India, in his large sample of drawings, and Werner (1948) also reported them. Hudson (cited by Deręgowski, 1962) found that illiterate Africans preferred chain drawings and that although African schoolchildren showed a lower preference for them than did adults, their preference was still greater than that of European schoolchildren.

Fortes (1940) described the figures drawn by his 6- to 16-year-old Tallensi children as a spatial or functional diagram of a person. He noted how the proportions of the figures seem to reflect the functional importance of various body parts. In the drawing of a man, for example, the fingers and the toes may be shown as prominently as the arms. Furthermore, there was no attempt to represent perspective or the three-dimensional qualities of a person, only in so far as the torso might be made "thick" by broadening out the vertical line into a crude rectangular or oval blob. Indeed, he suggested that we should think of these figures as *ideograms* rather than as pictures.

Although Western children prefer to draw their figures in a canonical orientation with each body part as far as possible occupying its own space (see Chapter 3), they none the less enclose some features within the contour of another. An example is the enclosure of the facial features

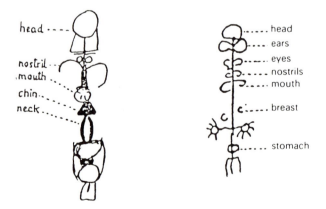

FIG. 7.5 "Chain" figures drawn by a girl aged 6 years from the Belgian Congo (left) and an Indian boy also aged 6 years from India (right). (From Paget, 1932.)

FIG. 7.6 Omission of a facial boundary. From left to right, figures drawn by a 7-year-old Iranian girl, a 9-year-old Kenyan girl, a 10-year-old boy from the Lunda tribe (Rhodesia) and a 9-year-old girl from the Bakongo tribe (Portuguese Congo). (From Paget, 1932.)

within the surrounding contour of the head. In my sample of 454 UK children's drawings between the ages of 2 years and 7 years 6 months, only three omitted the head contour; these children were aged 3 years, 4 years and 4 years 5 months. They all arranged the facial features in a spatially accurate way and then added legs below them; one child added arms to the legs and the other two added feet.

There are examples of other cultures in Paget's data in which the facial features are not enclosed by the head contour (see Fig. 7.6). In the chain structures described above, the head is placed above and separate from the facial features. But, even when some children arrange the facial features in a visually realistic way, they often omit the facial boundary in the same way as the three children in my data described above; whereas these three children were very young and were drawing tadpole or transitional figures, many of those in Paget's data were older and were actually drawing very detailed conventional figures. Paget also provides some examples of profile figures in which the facial features are placed separately to one side of the head region (see Fig. 7.6).

In the examples in which the head contour does not appear at all, it may be that the spatial arrangement of the facial features is sufficient to imply that the figure has a head. In cases in which the facial features and the head are drawn separately, it may be that the children simply think of these as separate parts. Furthermore, they might be reluctant to enclose the features within a contour because this might imply that the facial features are *inside* the head rather than on its outer surface (Cox, 1992).

Depiction of Racial/Cultural Features

One of the most notable differences between races is perhaps skin colour, and one might expect that children of different races would indicate this in their human figure drawings. But, according to Di Leo (1973, p. 21), both black and white children simply draw a contour for the face and do not colour it in to show the skin colour. A number of other researchers have made this observation. For example, Goodenough (1926) included 16 black children among her group of children, aged from 6 years 5 months to 14 years 5 months, and none of their figures had any facial shading or other racial features. In Dennis's (1966) collection of drawings from children in Cambodia, Greece, Iran, Israel, Japan, Lebanon, Mexico, Sweden, Taiwan, Turkey, UK, USA and the former West Germany, the figures appeared to depict white men in Western dress. Pfeffer (1984) found that 129 Yoruba schoolchildren in Nigeria, with a mean age of 8 years, generally avoided colouring in the skin areas of their figures, but, even if they did colour them in, they did not choose dark colours. Similarly, Papadakis-Michaelides (1989) found that among the 3200 figures drawn by 1600 children from five cultural backgrounds in the UK (English, Hindu, Muslim, Sikh and West Indian; aged 3 years 6 months to 11 years 6 months), only one figure was dark-skinned.

There are problems here regarding our expectation that different cultural groups should emphasise skin colour or a particular style of dress. To begin with, skin colour may not be something that people are particularly aware of, especially if their cultural group is fairly homogeneous. And, secondly, even if they are aware of it, they may not choose to display it in a drawing. Thus, a circle on a white page does not necessarily mean that the black child intends the region to be a white face any more than the white child does; it is simply a face. Similarly, if a white or a black child draws a figure on a blackboard with white chalk, the figure is simply a figure and not necessarily a black one. In fact, a major practical problem would arise if children were to colour in the face: it would be more difficult to make the facial features show up. An interesting study, suggested by Pfeffer (1984), would be to provide children with paper of different colours and then to observe their choices when asked to draw figures belonging to different racial groups.

A feature which could be drawn in different ways but which, unlike skin colour, would not have the same practical implications for the drawing is the nose. Although there are similarities among noses worldwide, there are also racial differences. Paget (1932) noted that the typical Chinese nose tends to be broad and thick, the Indian and Arab slender, and in the Burmese the wings of the nostrils are prominent. Do children reflect these physical differences in their choice of schema for the nose or are cultural differences in the drawings simply a reflection of a difference in children's choice among a set of conventional symbols? Paget provides some evidence that they do reflect racial differences in nose shape: the symbols ∪, ☐, △ and △ were frequently found among the drawings of Chinese children and φ was typically found in children's drawings in Egypt and Palestine. Although Paget does not specify a particular symbol for Burmese children, he none the less says that the nostrils are emphasised in over half of their full-face figures. Despite these differences, however, Paget is at pains to emphasise that there are many solutions to the problem of how best to depict a nose and that the variation of symbols adopted by children in most cultures is quite wide and may well be influenced by existing conventions or the children's own inventions.

Another racial/cultural difference which children might emphasise in their drawings is the hairstyle and dress of the figure. Again a number of studies have noted a lack of such distinguishing features (e.g. Dennis, 1966; Papadakis-Michaelides, 1989). This common finding may in part be explained by considering whether the group under consideration is a minority group within a larger culture. Where this is the case (e.g. Papadakis-Michaelides, 1989), it may be that children have not wished to draw attention to their cultural/racial origins and, in addition, many of them may not in fact normally dress in the traditional style. In cases in which the children have been tested in their country of origin, the depiction of cultural and racial features is sometimes much more common: Pfeffer (1984), for example, found that 25% of her Yoruba sample drew their

FIG. 7.7   Figure drawing by a 14-year-old Yoruba girl. (Reproduced with the permission of Dr Karen Pfeffer.)

figures in traditional dress, 40% drew African hairstyles and 50% drew African facial features (see Fig. 7.7).

A low frequency of "ethnic" features and dress of the figures does not necessarily mean that children cannot draw them. Indeed, when they are specifically asked to draw a certain cultural or racial type, then they have no hesitation or difficulty in doing so. Dennis (1966) reports that when he asked black and Indian children to draw a negro figure, they were easily able to depict negroid features and dress. Similarly, Frisch and Handler (1967) found that when their children were instructed to draw a negro person, 80% of black children's figures had noticeable negroid features.

There are other noticeable differences among different cultures in the way that certain body parts are drawn, which seem to be simply conventional differences and do not reflect any physical differences in shape among the people themselves. An example is the shape of the torso (see Fig. 7.8). When Western children first add the torso to their figures as a separate unit, they usually draw an oval region (see Chapter 3); they rarely draw a stick-like figure in which the torso is represented by a single vertical line. This is by no means universal, however. In some African groups, the torso may indeed be represented by a vertical line or be assumed in the space between two vertical lines extending from the head to the feet. In the chain drawings mentioned earlier, however, the torso is not represented at all except in as much as it is implied by the vertical axis of the figure and features such as arms, breasts and stomach.

In many societies, as well as those in the West, the torso is represented by an enclosed region, but this region is not always the same shape. In Paget's data, there are several examples of inverted triangular torsos among African children's drawings and Wilson and Wilson (1984) have observed the markedly rectangular torso found in many countries in Africa and the Middle East; in fact, they refer to this as the "Islamic" torso. In

FIG. 7.8 Regional differences in torso shape. From left to right, rectangular torso drawn by a Yoruba boy aged 10 years (reproduced with the permission of Dr Karen Pfeffer), triangular torsos drawn by a Bergdama boy from S.W. Africa (aged 7), a Herero-Hottentot boy from Namaland (aged 8) and a Bergdama boy (aged 10). (From Paget, 1932.)

FIG. 7.9   Rake-like hands and feet of figures drawn by a 9-year-old and a 10-year-old from India. (Reproduced with the permission of Dr Poonam Batra.)

a sample of Yoruba drawings collected by Karen Pfeffer in Nigeria, I found that the rectangular torso is very marked in the drawings of low-income children but is virtually absent from those in middle-income families.

In a study of the drawings of 54 rural 4- to 11-year-olds in India (Cox & Batra, n.d.), the shape of the torsos did not differ particularly from those seen in the drawings of 56 urban 3- to 6-year-olds nor those in UK children's drawings. What was very marked in the rural drawings, however, was the depiction of the hands and feet. Not only did more of these children add hands (93%) and feet (91%) to their figures compared with the urban children (71 and 66%, respectively), but they had a very characteristic rake-like style not seen among the urban children's drawings at all, nor among the UK children's drawings (see Fig. 7.9).

How Children Learn to Draw

In cultures in which there is no tradition of representing the human form in a drawing, children and indeed adults may at first scribble and experiment with the marks they make on the page. Rouma (1913) noticed that if children have had no experience of drawing, they quickly catch up with a small amount of practice, and Schubert (1930) remarked on the naturalistic quality of Orotchen children's drawings who had not even seen a picture up to 3 months before her study.

Unless they are given a ready-made conventional schema to copy, children and adults who are making their first attempts to draw a person must grapple on their own with the problem of how best the figure should be represented. It is interesting that on the whole the representational forms they produce bear at least some visual-spatial relationship to a real figure and are rarely arbitrary symbols, like the semi-circle used by the Walbiri. As children become more exposed to pictures and see the way that others draw, in school perhaps, they change their own schemes and often adopt a more conventional form. So, for example, the Walbiri children adopt the semi-circle used by the Walbiri women to stand for a person, Balinese children model their figures on those seen in traditional shadow puppet plays (Belo, 1955), and Western children's conventional figures have a distinctive "cottage-loaf" style (Paget, 1932). Thus, the cultural influence on drawings increases as young children or naive adults develop their skills and experience. Many studies have noted the difference between unschooled children's drawings and those of children who have received schooling. When Fortes (1940; 1981) and his wife collected some human figure drawings from the unschooled Tallensi during the period 1934–37, they also collected some from children at a nearby boarding school and found that the latter were much more European in style. Furthermore, in 1970, Fortes collected more drawings from the Tallensi settlement, this time from children aged between 5 and 13 years attending the local primary school and some of whom were the children and grandchildren of the original sample in the 1930s. These children drew in a European style, often depicting their figures in profile, and produced more skilful drawings than the boarding school children 35 years previously.

Peer Influence

Paget (1932) argues that the primary influence on children's drawings is not so much the adults' mode of representation but the way that other children draw, and he claims that this influence operates in a similar way to that on children's playground games (Opie & Opie, 1969): The schema for the whole body or for separate parts of it is simply observed and absorbed by succeeding generations of children.

   Wilson and Wilson (Wilson, 1985) have studied some of the drawings collected over the last 100 years from children in many different countries and have become fascinated by some of the features that seem to be particular to certain local areas. One example concerns the complicated trouser-legs drawn by a sample of Spanish-speaking Californian children between the years 1917 and 1923, which, given the amount of erasure in some of the drawings, must have been quite difficult to construct (see Fig. 7.10). Another example concerns the back-mounted arms drawn on the profile figures by children in the 1920s in one particular school in Los Angeles (see Fig. 7.11). Wilson also noted that Ricci (1887) had reported these back-mounted arms in his study in Italy 35–40 years earlier. Since this school in Los Angeles had received a large number of Italian

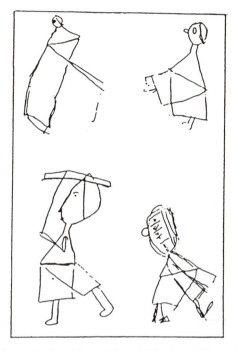

FIG. 7.10   Figures drawn by Spanish-speaking Californian children, 1917–23. (Top half reproduced with the permission of Professor Brent Wilson.)

immigrants during the 1920s, it is interesting to speculate that the style might have been imported by Italian immigrant children. I have looked through my samples of children's standard human figure drawings, figures who are running and figures drawn from a model seen in profile, but there is no case in which both arms of the figure are mounted on the back contour and no example of intersecting trouser-legs.

Presumably, the intersecting legs or the back-mounted arms must have been invented by one particular individual at some time and was then copied by others. Although it may have been the popularity of that person which prompted other children to copy the style, the persistence of the style over time needs further explanation. I suggest that it persists because it solves a particular representational problem in an apt way. As far as I know, there are no experimental studies which have sought to implant a particular style of drawing within a population of children and then to observe the extent to which it spreads within and outside that population and also how long it continues. This kind of study would be a useful test of Paget's (1932) claim regarding the way that drawing styles are passed on and could also serve to test my suggestion (Cox, 1992, p. 69) that normal children may become more susceptible to the drawing styles of

FIG. 7.11   Back-mounted arms drawn by Californian children in the 1920s (top, reproduced with the permission of Professor Brent Wilson) and by Italian children in the 1880s (bottom).

others when they have resolved the very basic problem of what lines can be used for and how a figure can be drawn. Although it appears to be extremely difficult to impose a conventional style of drawing the human figure on the young tadpole-drawer (see Chapter 2), it may be easier to change the style of older children who may be more open to wider social influences.

Implications for Our Understanding of Children's Drawings

Some researchers (e.g. Arnheim, 1974; Kellogg, 1969) have assumed that there is a universal aesthetic appeal in certain shapes and configurations and that this leads to a universal pattern of development in children's drawings. Kellogg has argued for a building-block sequence of development from simple to more complex "good forms" and claims that in drawing their first representational figures, children are more concerned with the balance of the form than with its visual similarity to a real figure. The evidence, however, does not sit happily with these claims (see Chapter 1). It appears that the pre-representational practice in the construction of detailed configuration is not actually necessary. Not all Western children progress through the sequence of steps put forward by Kellogg and those children in other cultures who have not had any experience of drawing before also draw representational forms and bypass many of these earlier stages.

Whereas some writers (e.g. Alland, 1983; Dennis, 1966; Deręgowski, 1980; Stratford & Mei Lan Au, 1988) recognise similarities among different cultures at the scribbling stage, they emphasise how the different figures characteristic of each culture appear soon after this stage of experimentation is over. We have seen how the Walbiri children adopt the simple symbol for a person used by the adults in their community and which bears no visual resemblance to a real person. Thus, it is not necessarily the case that children seek to find ways of representing the *visual* and *spatial* aspects of the human form. Goodnow's (1977) "search for equivalents" or Golomb's (1981) "search for meaning and likeness" are not necessarily universal issues in children's representation.

Nevertheless, children in most cultures do in fact draw figures which, though in many cases unusual in appearance to Western eyes, are composed of separate items each standing for different body parts. The parts they choose to draw may be very different, however. Whereas great emphasis in the West has been placed on the importance of the head, the pin-head figures of some African cultures seem to minimise its importance not only by reducing its size but also by omitting its facial features altogether. Conversely, many non-Western cultures include the genitalia in their figures when these are quite rare in Western children's drawings.

When the same body parts in the drawings are compared, there is a wide range of different depictions. In some cases, they appear to reflect a particular physical characteristic of the people, such as a slender nose as opposed to a broad nose; but in many other cases, the choice of line or shape seems unrelated to differences in physical characteristics. A body part such as the torso is a somewhat irregular object, which could be depicted in a number of different ways. For example, one might think of it primarily as a bulky object and that it might best be depicted by a bounded region (Willats, 1985; 1987), and indeed most Western children draw it in this way. However, we might also think of it as a long object, in which case a single vertical line, a wide vertical "stripe", or two vertically placed parallel lines bounding a central space might also be appropriate depictions. The smooth lumpiness of the torso might suggest a curvilinear shape, but the angular shoulders might suggest a more rectangular or an inverted triangular shape. In fact, we see all these solutions across a variety of different cultures.

The variety of solutions not only to the problem of how to represent the torso but of other body parts as well, raises a question regarding the way that children select each graphic form. Whereas, according to Willats (1985; 1987; see also Chapter 1), they consider (or describe to themselves) the whole volume of a body part and then select from their repertoire the form which best fits their description, it may be that, in contrast, they consider only the surface area that is projected to the eye. It is difficult to tease apart these different explanations, but it seems that some depictions of the torso (e.g. a space bounded on each side by a vertical line) might be best accounted for by the "surface" explanation rather than the volumetric one. It is possible, of course, that some children focus on the surface area, whereas others focus on the whole volume of the body part. In Western cultures, at least, there is reckoned to be a shift with age from focusing on volumetric body parts towards the surface appearance of the figure as seen from a particular point of view.

The query regarding the universality of striving towards visual realism applies not only to the way that individual body items are drawn, but also how different parts of the figure are fixed together. Whereas most Western children draw a contour for a head which encompasses the facial features, thereby achieving both visual and spatial equivalence to the real object, there are many examples from other cultures in which either the head is drawn as a separate item above the facial features or in which no contour for the head appears at all. Particularly notable are the chain figures in which there are no encompassing contours such as a head or a torso; features associated with these body sections (eyes, nose, mouth, breasts, stomach, etc.) are added on to a vertical line as the child progresses down the figure. Thus, there is some spatial—and to some extent visual—arrangement of the items, but they are not embedded into larger units. Presumably, in their thinking about the human figure, at least for the purposes of representing it, the children who draw these chain figures successively recall individual body items individually and separately as they move down the figure and do not think in terms of body items subsumed within larger units such as the head and the torso sections.

The cultural diversity of drawings of the human form suggests that there is no ideal way of representing the human figure but many possible solutions; cultural differences may be, to a large extent, simply a reflection of the different choices that people make regarding which body parts should be represented, how each part should be drawn and how they should be fixed together. Furthermore, these choices do not necessarily reflect different levels of cognitive functioning or intelligence, as some writers have assumed. In 1934, Fortes studied a group of Tallensi children in Northern Ghana (Fortes, 1940). In one task, the children were required to arrange some geometrical shapes in any way they chose. Whereas English children would arrange them into a pattern starting in the centre and working outwards, the younger Tallensi children simply put pieces down at random and the older ones, from about 11 and 12 upwards, sorted them into lines of different shapes. Apparently, when Fortes reported these results to Löwenfeld, the originator of the test, she said that they were exactly like the work of mental defectives. Yet, the Tallensi subjects could not be regarded by any criterion as mentally defective. Both in terms of their normal functioning within their society and on their performance on a series of non-verbal tests, Fortes concluded that they were not lacking in perceptual capabilities, memory or thought. He has argued that the differences in the way that different groups deal with the material is culturally related (Fortes, 1940; 1981). The Tallensi were unfamiliar with the materials themselves and had been given no directive as to what to do with them. Although it might be useful to evaluate children's drawings within the same culture, when the normal choice of body parts and the way in which they are drawn is known, it is clearly erroneous to assume that human figure drawings can be used as a culture-free test of intellectual maturity or intelligence across different cultures when the same criteria do not necessarily apply.

8 Overview

One of the reasons why people are interested in children's drawings and, in particular, their drawings of the human figure, is a curiosity about certain phenomena such as the tadpole form (see Chapter 2) and the transparency drawings (see Chapter 3), which are so strikingly characteristic of the younger child's drawings but rarely occur in the drawings of older children and adults. These kinds of phenomena have prompted a number of explanations, focusing on children's motor or perceptual skills, on their ability to construct mental representations, or on their ideas and intentions regarding an adequate pictorial representation.

A second strand of interest running through the literature is the potential usefulness of children's human figure drawings as an indicator of intelligence or intellectual maturity. As the sequence of stages outlined by Rouma (1913) shows, the developmental sequence in the way that figures are drawn was noted very early in the history of the study of children's drawings (see Introduction). Although not all children necessarily go through every stage, in the main the general pattern has remained uncontentious. Related to the use of the developmental sequence of human figure drawings as a guide to children's intellectual level is its use as an indicator of children's emotional development, based on the notion that deviations from the way that figures are typically drawn at a certain mental age might give a clue towards, or confirmation of, a child's temporary or even more enduring emotional difficulties.

A third interest in children's drawings concerns questions about their universality, which in turn raises questions about the mental processes and skills often assumed to be necessary or sufficient for creating a pictorial representation. Since most of the research on children's drawings has been carried out by Western researchers on the drawings of children in Western societies, it is tempting to assume that the well-documented and replicated findings are universal. That children and, indeed, adults in different cultures may devise other ways of representing the human figure is interesting not only to those concerned with questions about the different ways that objects can be represented, but also serves to check what might otherwise be assumed to be universal, developmental constraints on the skills and mental processes involved in the task.

In general, research has focused separately on the three broad areas of work mentioned above, although the findings in one area sometimes have relevance and implications for the ideas and assumptions in others. In this final chapter, I shall highlight some of the main issues arising from the previous chapters and, where applicable, make reference across the three main areas outlined above.

The Purpose of Scribbling

Some researchers (e.g. Bender, 1938; Harris, 1963) have claimed that the child who scribbles is simply enjoying the motor movement of the activity and, some time later, is experimenting with and practising a variety of movements and patterns. This early activity enables the child to gain greater control over the pencil so that he is better able to produce an intended line or shape rather than those which happen to appear as a result of his uncontrolled movements. Even when his control of the pencil is quite assured, however, some researchers, such as Kellogg (1969), have maintained that the young child is still not concerned with producing representational forms but with forms which are aesthetically well-balanced. Indeed, when asked what they are drawing, many children will answer that they are "just scribbling" or "making a pattern".

None the less, young children are aware that drawings are or can be representational and, sometimes, will announce a topic prior to or during their own scribbling. Moreover, when they ask an adult or an older child to draw something, they know that a visual likeness to the object will be brought about even though they cannot achieve it for themselves.

Research, mainly based on careful observation of individual children's scribbling activities, has revealed that the change from a supposed pre-representational stage to a representational stage is not so clear-cut as was previously thought (see Chapter 1). Even when a scribble bears no visual likeness to an object, it may be the movement of the object or action of the event which the child is simulating. These *action* or *gestural representations*, as they have been called (Matthews, 1984; Wolf & Perry, 1988), seem to occur, in some children at least, before they are able to capture the more enduring visual likeness of an object.

One account of how children come to realise that their own scribbles can capture something of the visual likeness of an object is that they recognise things in their scribbles by accident. This recognition of objects, termed *fortuitous realism* by Luquet (1913), presumably stimulates children to set about their subsequent drawings in an intentional and planned way. Although some children sometimes do recognise objects in their scribbles, there is no available evidence as far as I know that they subsequently attempt to draw these same "fortuitous" objects in an intentional way. For example, when they are asked to draw a person or decide for themselves that they want to draw a human form, we have no evidence that it is only those children who have already "seen" a person in their scribbles who will be successful. In fact, the likelihood is that when children are faced with this representational task, they will have to construct a schema for the first time and, at that point, are faced with the problem of how to make it look recognisable.

It appears, then, that although scribbling may sometimes be representational, in the sense that it simulates the movement of an object or an event, and also that children may occasionally recognise objects in their scribbles, when they are faced with the task of drawing a visually recognisable form, they are in the position of constructing or finding a *new* graphic form. Although the activity of scribbling may help the child to gain some control over the pencil and may provide an opportunity to practise various movements and graphic forms, this activity is not a necessary precursor to the production of representational drawing; nor for that matter is the occurrence of fortuitous realism when the child by chance recognises certain objects in his scribbles. This conclusion regarding the status of scribbling is also supported by studies in a variety of different cultural groups—children or adults who have not previously had the opportunity to draw do not need to go through an extensive, or indeed any, scribbling stage in order to produce some kind of recognisable, representational figure (see Chapter 7).

The Tadpole Figure

The earliest recognisable human forms in children's drawings are usually the minimal "tadpole" figures, often consisting of only a head and some legs, and there have been a variety of views expressed about the reasons for this form. From the results of a number of studies (discussed in Chapter 2) we can discount some of these; for example, Arnheim's (1974) claim that the tadpole form is a complete but undifferentiated figure, Freeman's (1975; 1980) view that it is the result of the child's limited capacity to recall

all the main body parts, and Golomb's (1981) claim that children simply prefer to draw a minimal figure.

It is clear that the tadpole-drawer is quite knowledgeable about the human figure but is constrained to some extent in the way he is able to draw it. In particular, although he knows the spatial layout of the various body parts, he has not yet devised a schema for the torso and, secondly, often forgets to include the arms. When the experimenter mentions the torso at an appropriate point in a dictation task, the tadpole-drawer still fails to draw a conventional figure; however, when a ready-made schema for the torso is provided for him, the tadpole-drawer is able to include it in the correct position within his figure (manikin task). As far as the arms are concerned, these are included if the tadpole-drawer is reminded about them (dictation task) or is given ready-made arms in a manikin task. Schemas for the head and the legs of the figure are probably drawn first because the child fixes his attention on these body parts first of all, the reason being, as a number of writers (Barnes, 1894; Golomb, 1988; Luquet, 1913; Ricci, 1887) have claimed, that the head and the legs are, for the child, the most important and definitive features of the human form. This assumption may only apply to children in Western societies, however; it seems that the production of the tadpole form may not be universal (see Chapter 7), and if this is true then it follows that the primary importance of the head and the legs in the representation of the human form is also not necessarily universal. In some other cultures, the head and legs, although they may be represented, are not always given the same prominence in the figure as in the Western tadpole, and other features, such as the torso, the hands and the genitalia, may be particularly exaggerated.

The Internal Model

A number of researchers have argued that children do not draw from real objects but from an internal model (Luquet, 1913; 1927). The exact nature of such an internal model is unclear. Nevertheless, a predominant notion regarding the model is that when he intends to draw an object, say the human figure, a child conjures up a mental image of it based on his knowledge of the figure. This notion of the model is probably the most common in the literature on children's drawing, although it is sometimes implicit rather than explicitly stated.

An important issue is whether, when the child conjures up such an internal model, this model is complete in the sense that it reflects everything the child actually knows about the object. Thus, even though the tadpole-drawer can recognise and name the main body parts of the human figure—head, torso, legs and arms—do all of these features appear in the internal model? A number of writers (e.g. Barnes, 1894; Kerschensteiner, 1905; Luquet, 1913; Ricci, 1887) believe that they do not and that the child captures only the ones most definitive of the human form, namely the head and the legs. The subsequent relationship between the model and the drawing is deemed to be direct, i.e. all the features in the internal model are reproduced on the page. However, if such a model is thought to be relatively stable, it is difficult to explain why some children are not very consistent in what they draw, sometimes adding and sometimes omitting body parts and sometimes even drawing tadpole figures, transitionals and conventional forms on the same page (e.g. Eng, 1931).

Other researchers state or, at least imply, that the internal model is complete (Arnheim, 1974; Freeman, 1975; and possibly Golomb, 1988). For Freeman and possibly for Golomb, the child's internal model is regarded as being complete and segmented into its constituent parts. In Arnheim's case, although the model is considered to be complete, it is not entirely differentiated, so that the head and torso, for example, may be fused together rather than separated into two distinct units. Since the internal model, at least in Freeman's account, is thought to be complete and differentiated, there must be some intervening process which prevents the complete figure from being reproduced on the page. Freeman assumes that the child should be able to draw each body part (i.e. can or could devise a particular way of drawing it), but he argues that the child's problem is in recalling all of the body parts in the correct sequence.

Although it is less clear whether Golomb postulates an internal model of the same kind, at least she assumes that the tadpole-drawer has considerable knowledge of the human figure, but she maintains that the child is not intent on drawing everything she knows. Rather, the child intends the tadpole form as an apt if minimal representation of the human form. In Golomb's case, as in Freeman's, there is no direct mapping from the internal model of knowledge onto what the child actually draws; for Golomb, the child's intentions intervene.

The results of the various studies discussed in Chapter 2 have some implications for these various positions regarding the internal model. The fact that tadpole-drawers are particularly entrenched in their way of drawing the human figure, despite the various attempts to alleviate the production-load of the drawing task, suggests that their difficulty is not simply a problem of recalling the body parts in the correct order (Freeman), nor is it simply a preference for drawing a tadpole form rather than a conventional form (Golomb). Furthermore, there is evidence that the tadpole is not an undifferentiated figure (Arnheim).

That we can discount, or at least doubt, these various explanations does not mean that we have to accept the earlier account that the child's internal model is incomplete. There is a further possibility, that the internal model is complete but that the child has not necessarily worked out ways of drawing each part all at once. It may be that she devises graphic forms for the most salient features first (i.e. the head and the legs) and only later turns to the other, perhaps less important, body parts. In this account, then, the internal model is complete but the child acts differentially on working out graphic forms for different body parts and this process, in turn, is determined by which body parts the child considers particularly salient or interesting.

Although the data presented in Chapter 2 lend support to this explanation detailed above, it must be pointed out that the main evidence comes from a manikin task which requires the child to construct a figure from ready-made pieces rather than to draw a figure. Since tadpole-drawers are able to construct conventional figures using these pieces, it is suggested that their internal model of the human form is complete and, presumably, guides their construction. Now, it may indeed be the case that the child generates the same complete model in a drawing task as in a manikin task but, in the drawing task in particular, has some problems in translating the model onto the page. Alternatively, it could be that the internal model generated in each of these tasks is different. Perhaps the child really does conjure up a minimal model (head and legs) when he sets out on the drawing task, but in the manikin task perhaps the sight of all the recognisable body parts prompts him to conjure up a more detailed model than usual. The suggestion here, then, is that children may not always generate the same internal model but that different tasks may prompt them to generate different models, some more detailed than others. So, they must possess enough underlying knowledge on which to base the most detailed figure they can produce. Although the exact way that this underlying knowledge itself is stored or represented cannot be ascertained from the data presented in this chapter, it may be, for example, that it is stored in some propositional form (e.g. Olson & Bialystock, 1983), which is then converted into a picture, in varying degrees of detail, depending on the child's perception of the task he is being asked to perform.

The Search for Equivalents

The task faced by young drawers may best be described as trying to capture something of the likeness of a real object. This process, originally mentioned by Arnheim (1974), has been characterised by Goodnow (1977) as a "search for equivalents" and has also been called a "search for meaning and likeness" by Golomb (1981). It involves the child in selecting or constructing a schema which will be, at least minimally, adequate in suggesting or evoking the real object.

One solution to the problem of finding suitable forms of representation is for children to use the forms already available in their repertoire (Kellogg, 1969). The evidence for this claim, however, is unconvincing, since many children do not produce the forms thought to be precursors of the human form and, indeed, appear to invent a completely new form when faced with this task.

Willats (1985; 1987) has put forward an alternative explanation of how the young child might set about the task of finding graphic equivalents for the various body parts of the human figure he wishes to represent (see Chapter 1). Although each body part is an object which exists in three spatial dimensions, each one may be characterised in a particular way; so, for example, the head might be thought of as a bulky object which is equally extended in all three dimensions, a hand might be regarded more as a flat surface extending in two dimensions, the limbs as long things extending mainly in one dimension, and the pupils of the eyes as points extending in no particular dimension at all. According to Willats, the child then selects from his graphic repertoire the lines or shapes most appropriate for each of these. For the very young child, the choice is largely confined to single lines, roughly circular shapes (called *regions* by Willats) and also dots. A region is the most appropriate for the head of the figure and lines for the limbs.

A limitation of Willat's account is its lack of universality. It seems an attractive proposition that the head should be thought of as a bulky item and that therefore a large region would be chosen to denote it. Drawings from other cultures, however, such as the pin-head figures of the Tallensi (Fortes, 1940) and the Kalahari Bushmen (Reuning & Wortley, 1973), indicate that the head is not universally regarded in this way (see Chapter 7). Similarly, although in Western cultures when the torso is included in the figure it is typically represented by a relatively large elongated region, again reflecting the large bulk of the torso, in some other cultures it is represented by a vertical line or a thickened vertical band. These differences in the way body parts are typically depicted suggests that they can be conceptualised in different ways and that children reflect these differences in their drawings. It is not clear, however, why different cultures should emphasise different aspects or characteristics of particular body parts.

The relative intransigence of the Western tadpole-drawer (see Chapter 2) might lead one to suppose that the search for successful or realistic graphic schemas comes about through the child's own internal desire for change rather than from external pressure. However, the fact that children within a particular culture tend to produce a similar form—tadpole figures in Western societies, a non-pictorial semi-circle among the Walbiri, more linear forms in African groups—suggests that even if they do not receive direct tuition in how to draw they may be influenced, none the less, by the prevailing graphic forms around them. Thus, the cultural differences in the particular body parts selected and in the way they are drawn and put together suggests that, in their search for suitable schemas, children are not wholly original; rather, their search for a realistic schema (as advocated by Fenson, 1985; Luquet, 1913; 1927) is tempered by, or interacts with, their absorption of a wider, cultural influence.

Constraints on Change

The early tadpole forms drawn by children in Western societies are typically very minimal and, as I have already pointed out, often resistant to change. One reason why the young child might not readily change her graphic form was put forward by Willats (1985). He has argued that the young child has a very limited repertoire of lines and regions which can be used to represent the various body parts of the human figure. In particular, although a child may be able to vary the size of a region, she cannot alter its shape; she is more or less constrained to drawing a roughly circular region. The elaboration of the child's human figure drawing depends on her being able to modify the limited repertoire of lines and regions, and in particular being able to alter the shape of a region. Without this ability, the child will not be able to show the differences between different body parts.

It is difficult to accept this supposed limitation, however. Even though the child might have only a very few ways of representing different body parts, their spatial position in relation to the figure as a whole would indicate what they are meant to be. Children at this age are quite knowledgeable about the spatial layout of the human form, as the results of a manikin task testify, and it has also been noted by Fortes (1940), for example, that in some cultures human figure drawings appear more like a spatial or functional diagram of the human figure rather than a visual likeness. Thus, a limited repertoire should not necessarily be a hindrance to adding more body parts; the spatial position of a body part would indicate its identity. Having said this, however, the child may be reluctant to use a particular graphic form like a circular region if the body part in question is, as far as she is concerned, a very different shape. A child might, for example, perceive a foot as a long, flat object but be reluctant to use either a single line or a circular region to represent it.

Even when children move on to drawing conventional figures, these forms are rigid and stylised. An explanation has been offered by Karmiloff-Smith (1986; 1990): The production of the schema is likened to a program which the young child "runs" in a fixed way and cannot alter, only in so far as extra items or omitted items occur at the beginning or at the end of the program; older children can manipulate their program and can interrupt it and modify it at any point. As Spensley (1990) has found, however, young children are in fact much more flexible than this view would suggest; they can, for example, interrupt their normal drawing procedure to add a beard to their figure. Based on this finding and also on her inability to replicate Karmiloff-Smith's results, Spensley concludes that there is little support for a fixed procedure explanation.

A particular constraint which has found considerable support, however, is the child's level of planning ability. In Chapter 3, I presented evidence which shows how young children often overestimate the size of the head of their figures if, for example, the head is drawn first and occupies too much space or if it is to contain a number of facial details.

Paying attention to the planning of a scene is also important for older children, who are more concerned to draw from life or, at least, to draw a scene as if it had been viewed from a particular position (Luquet, 1913; 1927). Such planning necessitates the need to imagine how the scene would look from a particular viewpoint and to consider which parts would be obscured from view. According to Piaget and Inhelder (1956), children do not begin to develop this ability to take a point of view *vis-à-vis* a scene until about the age of 7 years, although there is some evidence that children younger than this do have some awareness of different viewpoints (Cox, 1991). But, without some consideration of how the scene should look from a certain perspective, the child may end up with a transparency drawing in which hidden objects or parts of objects are made visible, often overlapping the contours of other parts of the scene.

An ability to imagine what the scene should look like does not inevitably ensure success, however. A child may be able to do this but still not be able to plan the scene appropriately. Often the order of drawing the objects in a scene or the body parts of a figure has to be done differently from what might seem to be the "logical" order (Cox, 1992). For example, one might be tempted to draw a torso first and then attach the arms to it, but if the figure is to be drawn in profile this may result in a transparency. Thus, a transparency may occur as a result of poor planning. A more realistic picture can be produced if the arms—or those parts closer to the viewer—are drawn first and then the broken contours of the torso are fitted in around them.

Stages of Realism

There is a great deal of support for the claim that children generally present their figures in a *canonical* orientation, i.e. the figure is drawn facing the viewer so that the most characteristic view of each body part is displayed (see Chapter 3). It appears that the reason for the prevalence of the canonical view is not a concern that the figure should be photographically realistic, but that it should be optimally recognisable. This concern with producing a recognisable figure which displays its most distinguishing features has been called *intellectual realism* and is contrasted with *visual realism* (Luquet, 1913; 1927), a concern with representing a more fleeting snapshot of the way a figure happens to look from a particular angle of view. In order to present each body part in the most characteristic way, children also seek to arrange the figure so that body parts do not cross one another and are very reluctant to violate this "each to its own space" rule (Goodnow, 1977). Even when they are required to observe a figure in profile before drawing this view, they still seek to arrange the figure so as to avoid overlaps.

Luquet's (1913; 1927) account of the development of children's drawings has often been interpreted as advocating a *stage-like progression* from intellectual to visual realism, stage-like in the sense that a child is in one, and only one, stage at a time and that the second stage (namely, visual realism) reflects a more complex and mature cognitive structure. This categorisation of children's thinking was characteristic of the way that Piaget viewed child development in general (e.g. Piaget, 1950; 1953) and, since it was Piaget and Inhelder (1956) who referred extensively to Luquet's work on drawings, it may be that it is *their* notion of stage rather than Luquet's which has predominated. In actual fact, the interpretation of "stage" even in Piagetian theory has been problematic (see, for example, Brown & Desforges, 1977; Flavell, 1971) and it is by no means clear how flexible it was intended to be. Luquet himself, as Costall (1989) has pointed out, actually discussed the developmental shift much more in terms of children's *tendencies* to focus on intellectual or visual realism rather than as a shift from one clear-cut stage to another.

Even though many, if not most, children seem to draw in a consistent way over at least a short period of time, a more flexible notion of "stage" helps us to explain why some children sometimes draw their figures in very different ways, on the same day or even on the same piece of paper. Notable examples are children who draw tadpole figures and conventional figures as well as transitional figures. Clearly, this mixture cannot be accounted for by some general cognitive constraint; these children are obviously capable of drawing what we might consider to be the most advanced or mature form, namely the conventional figure. That they sometimes do not do so may reflect temporary lapses in attention or their varying concerns about what they are trying to achieve.

Luquet pointed out that, even though the younger child's concerns tend towards depicting the invariant characteristics of the object rather than its fleeting visual appearance, around the age of approximately 6 years children are aware of the potential conflict between different ways of representing an object. Thus, the young child is not prohibited by some developmental-cognitive constraint from considering the way that a figure appears from a certain viewpoint and, indeed, in some circumstances might be clearly aware of a particularly unusual view. We now have considerable evidence in support of Luquet's position. Although young children—even younger than the age of 6 years—often do present what has often been termed an intellectually realistic view of an object or a scene, under some circumstances they will represent a scene in a visually realistic way (e.g. Cox, 1981; 1985; Davis, 1983; 1985; Ingram, 1983; Ingram & Butterworth, 1989). And, indeed, older children and adults sometimes produce intellectually realistic rather than visually realistic representations (e.g. Cox, 1986).

Use of Drawings for Diagnostic Purposes

One of the primary interests in children's drawings of the human figure has been their use as diagnostic aids. Since it has been widely recognised that the details included in children's drawings of the human figure increase as their mental age increases, a test based on human figure drawings seemed an ideal tool for diagnosing a child's level of intelligence or intellectual maturity (see Chapter 4). As a very broad guide to intellectual level, there seems to be little dispute, as tests such as the Goodenough–Harris "Draw-a-Man" test (Harris, 1963) and Koppitz's "Draw-a-Person" test (Koppitz, 1968) have reasonably good reliability and validity. Unlike some of the detailed batteries of tests, however, such as the Wechsler Intelligence Scale for Children (Wechsler, 1974) or the British Ability Scales (Elliott, Murray, & Pearson, 1983), tests based on children's drawing of the human figure do not test specific kinds of abilities and therefore can do no more than be a very general guide.

Despite the frequently reported correlation between the increase in the inclusion of body parts and mental age, there are problems concerning children's intentions when drawing their figures which might make us wary of setting too much store by tests based on human figure drawings. Since there is a bias in the scoring towards the number of body parts added to the figure rather than towards the structure of the figure, the test may not reflect a particular child's true ability. So, for example, a detailed tadpole figure might receive a higher score than a conventional figure even though, in general, conventional figures are drawn by older children and are considered to be more mature forms. Similarly, a child who is experimenting with contoured figures or profile forms may be more interested in the outline of the figure rather than in adding more details to it. Another test, such as Raven's Matrices (Raven, Raven, & Court, 1991), which would not be subject to the same kinds of problems, might be preferred.

The use of children's drawings of the human figure as indicators of personality or emotional adjustment is similarly problematic (see Chapter 5). Again, as a very broad indicator, drawings collected under controlled conditions probably do give a very general idea. There is some evidence that certain clinical groups display more emotional indicators in their drawings than do normal children. However, there is no evidence that, for example, the omission of a certain body part or the way that it is drawn reflects a specific type of problem.

A major concern regarding the diagnostic use of children's human figure drawings is the often-made assumption that the task is culture-free. This assumption is based on claims that the way the human figure is represented is universal. As I have discussed, particularly in Chapter 7, the evidence from a variety of cross-cultural studies shows that this is not true: Adults and children in different cultures represent the human figure in different ways, both in the way that individual body parts are drawn and in the way that the whole figure is constructed. Furthermore, people in different societies have different concerns about the importance not only of different parts of the human figure but of the figure as a whole in relation to other objects and animals in a wider context. These differences among societies and indeed between boys and girls within Western societies (see Chapter 6) are reflected in the ways the drawings of the human figure develop. It is clearly invalid to take a scoring system based on a known accumulation of detail in one society and apply it to another group in which the developmental pattern is unknown. Even in the Western context, it has been recognised (e.g. Harris, 1963) that a different set of norms should be available for boys and for girls and yet concern regarding comparisons among cultural groups, which might arguably be more widely disparate, has rarely been voiced.

Universality of Drawings

Despite the claims for the universality of the way children's drawings develop (e.g. Kellogg, 1969), the evidence is not convincing (see Chapter 7). Although some of the pre-representational designs described by Kellogg have been found in a variety of different cultures and although a number of cross-cultural studies have shown that some children and, indeed, adults who have not drawn before produce tadpole figures, these forms are not found everywhere. In some cases, children and adults to whom drawing is a novel task have quickly or even immediately drawn a representational figure without first going through a sequence of pre-representational forms or producing the tadpole form. Furthermore, although their drawings may have shown some visual or spatial resemblance to a human figure, they have often been very different from those produced in Western cultures or in Western-educated groups within their own societies.

As I have already outlined, the large head, often with facial features, so characteristic of the early drawings of children in Western societies, is replaced in some cultures by a small "pin-head" with no facial features at all. In contrast, the torso which is omitted in the Western tadpole figure may be more detailed and prominent. Similarly, the arms and hands which are also frequently absent in Western tadpole forms are often exaggerated in the human figure drawings in other cultures. Clearly, if the head and the legs are definitive features of the human form for children in Western societies, this should not be taken as true for all children. The choice of particular body parts and the emphasis placed on them in a drawing may reflect different cultural concerns and values in different societies (Court, 1989). Children in Western societies who have been exposed to pictorial representations of the human form through books, cartoons, advertising, and so on, may already be predisposed to portray them in certain ways— emphasising the head and facial features, for example—whereas children in some other cultures may not have been influenced by this pervasive pictorial environment and will therefore not share the same experiences and predispositions; their solutions to the problem of how a person might best be represented in a picture may be very different.

References

Adler, P.T. (1971). Ethnic and socio-economic status differences in human figure drawings. *Journal of Consulting and Clinical Psychology*, *36*, 344–354.

Alland, A. (1983). *Playing with form*. New York: Columbia University Press.

Ames, L.B. (1943). The Gesell incomplete man test as a differential indicator of average and superior behaviour in preschool children. *Journal of Genetic Psychology*, *62*, 217–274.

Ames, L.B. (1945). Free drawing and completion drawing: A comparative study of preschool children. *Journal of Genetic Psychology*, *66*, 161–165.

Ames, L.B. & Ilg, F.L. (1963). The Gesell incomplete man test as a measure of developmental status. *Genetic Psychology Monographs*, *68*, 247–307.

Arazos, A. & Davis, A. (1989). Young children's representation of gender in drawings. Presented at the *British Psychological Society Developmental Section Annual Conference*, Guildford, September.

Arnheim, R. (1974). *Art and visual perception*, 2nd edn. Berkeley, CA: University of California Press.

Barnard, B.M. & Freeman, N.H. (1983). Regras infantis nos desenhos de aldatos mentalmente perturbados. *Analise Psicologica*, *1*, 177–182.

Barnes, E. (1894). The art of little children. *Pedagogical Seminary*, *3*, 302–307.

Barrett, M.D. & Light, P.H. (1976). Symbolism and intellectual realism in children's drawings. *British Journal of Educational Psychology*, *46*, 198–202.

Bassett, E.M. (1977). Production strategies in the child's drawing. In G. Butterworth (Ed.), *The child's representation of the world*. New York: Plenum Press.

Bee, H.L. & Walker, R.S. (1968). Experimental modification of the lag between perceiving and performing. *Psychonomic Science*, *11*, 127–128.

Belo, J. (1955). Balinese children's drawings. In M. Mead & M. Wolfenstein (Eds), *Childhood in contemporary cultures*. Chicago, IL: Chicago University Press.

Bender, L. (1938). *A visual motor gestalt test and its clinical use*. Research Monographs No. 3. New York: American Orthopsychiatric Association.

Bennett, V. (1964). Does the size of figure reflect self-concept? *Journal of Consulting Psychology*, *28*, 285–286.

Berman, S. & Laffal, J. (1953). Body type and figure drawing. *Journal of Clinical Psychology*, *9*, 368–370.

Bradbury, R.J. & Papadakis-Michaelides, E. (1990). Gender differences in children's human figure drawings. Presented at the *IVth European Conference on Developmental Psychology*, University of Stirling, August.

Brittain, W.L. & Chien, Y.-C. (1983). Relationship between preschool children's ability to name body parts and their ability to construct a man. *Perceptual and Motor Skills, 57*, 19–24.

Brown, G. & Desforges, C. (1977). Piagetian psychology and education: Time for revision. *British Journal of Educational Psychology, 47*, 7–17.

Brown, D.G. & Tolor, A. (1957). Human figure drawings as indicators of sexual identification and inversion. *Perceptual and Motor Skills, 7*, 199–211.

Brundege, B. & Fisher, E. (1990). Old masters: Turning stone into spirit. Cape Dorset hunters carve a stunning record of their lives on the land. *Equinox, 9*, 36–50.

Buck, J.N. (1948). The HTP test. *Journal of Clinical Psychology, 4*, 151–159.

Burgess, A.W., McCausland, M.P., & Wolbert, W.A. (1981). Children's drawings as indicators of sexual trauma. *Perspectives in Psychiatric Care, 19*, 50–58.

Buros, O.K. (Ed.) (1972) *The seventh mental measurement yearbook*, Vol. 1. Highland Park, NJ: The Gryphon Press.

Burt, C. (1921). *Mental and scholastic tests*. London: King and Son.

Canadian Eskimo Arts Council (1971). *Scupturel Inuit*. Toronto: University of Toronto Press.

Clegg, F. (1982). *Simple statistics*. Cambridge: Cambridge University Press.

Cooke, E. (1886). Our art teaching and child nature. *London Journal of Education*, January, pp. 12–15.

Coopersmith, S. (1967). *The antecedents of self-esteem*. San Francisco, CA: Freeman.

Coopersmith, S., Sakai, D., Beardslee, B., & Coopersmith, A. (1976). Figure drawing as an expression of self-esteem. *Journal of Personality Assessment, 46*, 371–375.

Costall, A. (1989). Another look at Luquet: Stages in our understanding of children's drawings. Paper presented at the *British Psychology Society Developmental Section Annual Conference*, University of Surrey, Guildford, September.

Cotterill, A. & Thomas, G.V. (1990). Children's production and perception of drawings of emotionally significant topics. Poster presented at the *IVth European Conference on Developmental Psychology*, University of Stirling, August.

Court, E. (1989). Drawing on culture: The influence of culture on children's drawing performance in rural Kenya. *Journal of Art and Design Education, 8*, 65–88.

Cox, M.V. (1981). One thing behind another: Problems of representation in children's drawings. *Educational Psychology, 1*, 275–287.

Cox, M.V. (1985). One object behind another: Young children's use of array-specific or view-specific representations. In N.H. Freeman & M.V. Cox (Eds), *Visual order: The nature and development of pictorial representation*. Cambridge: Cambridge University Press.

Cox, M.V. (1986). Cubes are difficult things to draw. *British Journal of Developmental Psychology, 4*, 341–345.

Cox, M.V. (1989). Children's drawings. In D.J. Hargreaves (Ed.), *Children and the arts*. Milton Keynes: Open University Press.

Cox, M.V. (1991). *The child's point of view*, 2nd edn. Hemel Hempstead: Harvester Wheatsheaf/New York: Guilford Press.

Cox, M.V. (1992). *Children's drawings*. Harmondsworth: Penguin.

Cox, M.V. & Batra, P. (n.d.). *The position of the torso in children's drawings of the human figure in the UK and in India*. Unpublished manuscript, University of York.

Cox, M.V. & Bayraktar, R. (1989). A cross-cultural study of children's human figure drawings. Presented at the *Tenth Biennial Conference of the International Society for the Study of Behavioural Development*, University of Jyväskylä, Finland, July.

Cox, M.V. & Howarth, C. (1989). The human figure drawings of normal children and those with severe learning difficulties. *British Journal of Developmental Psychology, 7*, 333–339.

Cox, M.V. & Jarvis, G. (n.d.). *Young children's "tadpole" drawings: The location of the torso*. Unpublished manuscript, University of York.

Cox, M.V. & Parkin, C. (1986). Young children's human figure drawing: Cross-sectional and longitudinal studies. *Educational Psychology, 6*, 353–368.

Craddick, R.A. (1961). Size of Santa Claus drawings as a function of the time before and after Christmas. *Journal of Psychological Studies, 12*, 121–125.

Craddick, R.A. (1963). Size of Hallowe'en witch drawings prior to, on and after Hallowe'en. *Perceptual and Motor Skills, 16*, 235–238.

Dalby, J.T. & Vale, H.L. (1977). Self-esteem and children's human figure drawings. *Perceptual and Motor Skills, 44*, 1279–1282.

Darwin, C. (1877). A biographical sketch of an infant. *Mind, 11*, 286–294.

Davis, A.M. (1983). Contextual sensitivity in young children's drawings. *Journal of Experimental Child Psychology, 35*, 478–486.

Davis, A.M. (1985). The canonical bias: Young children's drawings of familiar objects. In N.H. Freeman & M.V. Cox (Eds), *Visual order: The nature and development of pictorial representation*. Cambridge: Cambridge University Press.

Dégallier, A. (1905). Note psychologique sur les Negres Pahouins. *Archives de Psychologie, 4*, 362–368.

Delatte, J.G. & Hendrickson, N.J. (1982). Human figure drawing size as a measure of self-esteem. *Journal of Personality Assessment, 46*, 603–606.

Dennis, W. (1960). The human figure drawings of Bedouins. *Journal of Social Psychology, 52*, 209–219.

Dennis, W. (1966). *Group values through children's drawings*. New York: John Wiley.

Deręgowski, J.B. (1962). Preference for chain-type drawings in Zambian domestic servants and primary school children. *Psychologia Africana, 12*, 172–180.

Deręgowski, J.B. (1980). *Illusions, patterns and pictures: A cross-cultural perspective*. London: Academic Press.

Di Leo, J.H. (1970). *Young children and their drawings*. New York: Brunner Mazel.

Di Leo, J.H. (1973). *Children's drawings as diagnostic aids*. New York: Brunner Mazel.

Du Bois, C. (1944). *The people of Alor: A social-psychological study of an East Indian island*. Minneapolis: University of Minnesota Press.

Dziurawiec, S. & Deręgowski, J.B. (1992). "Twisted perspective" in young children's drawings. *British Journal of Developmental Psychology, 10*, 35–49.

Eames, C.M.A., Barrett, M.D., & McKee, S. (1990). Task demands versus stage theory in children's human figure drawing. Paper presented at the *IVth European Conference on Developmental Psychology*, University of Stirling, August.

Earl, C.J.C. (1933). The human figure drawing of feeble-minded adults. *Proceedings of the American Association of Mental Deficiency, 38*, 107–120.

Elkonin, D.B. (1957). The physiology of higher nervous activity and child psychology. In B. Simon (Ed.), *Psychology in the Soviet Union*. Palo Alto, CA: Stanford University Press.

Elliott, C.D., Murray, D.J., & Pearson, L.S. (1983). *British ability scales*. Windsor: NFER-Nelson.

Eng, H. (1931). *The psychology of children's drawings*. London: Routledge and Kegan Paul.

Fenson, L. (1985). The transition from construction to sketching in children's drawings. In N.H. Freeman & M.V. Cox (Eds), *Visual order: The nature and development of pictorial representation*. Cambridge: Cambridge University Press.

Flavell, J.H. (1971). Stage-related properties of cognitive development. *Cognitive Psychology*, *2*, 421–453.

Ford, C.H. (1977). Perception and projection of size, gender identity and self esteem in human figure drawings of young children. University of Texas, Austin. *Dissertation Abstracts International*, *38*, 7A, 4090.

Ford, M.A., Stern, D.D., & Dillon, D.J. (1974). Performance of children ages 3 to 5 on a draw a person task: Sex differences. *Perceptual and Motor Skills*, *38*, 1188.

Fortes, M. (1940). Children's drawings among the Tallensi. *Africa*, *13*, 239–295.

Fortes, M. (1981). Tallensi children's drawings. In B. Lloyd & J. Gay (Eds), *Universals of human thought*. Cambridge: Cambridge University Press.

Fox, T. & Thomas, G.V. (1990). Children's drawings of an anxiety-eliciting topic: Effect on size of the drawing. *British Journal of Clinical Psychology*, *29*, 71–81.

Fox, T. & Thomas, G.V. (n.d.). *Does the importance of the topic affect the size of children's figure drawings?* Unpublished manuscript, University of Birmingham.

Freeman, N.H. (1972). Process and product in children's drawing. *Perception*, *1*, 123–140.

Freeman, N.H. (1975). Do children draw men with arms coming out of the head? *Nature*, *254*, 416–417.

Freeman, N.H. (1980). *Strategies of representation in young children*. London: Academic Press.

Freeman, N.H. & Hargreaves, S. (1977). Directed movements and the body-proportion effect in pre-school children's human figure drawings. *Quarterly Journal of Experimental Psychology*, *29*, 227–235.

Frisch, R.G. & Handler, L. (1967). Differences in negro and white drawings: A cultural interpretation. *Perceptual and Motor Skills*, *24*, 667–670.

Gardner, H. (1980). *Artful scribbles*. London: Jill Norman.

Gellert, E. (1968). Comparison of children's self drawings with their drawings of other persons. *Perceptual and Motor Skills*, *26*, 125–138.

Gesell, A. (1925). *The mental growth of the pre-school child*. New York: Macmillan.

Ghent, L. (1961). Form and its orientation: A child's-eye view. *American Journal of Psychology*, *74*, 177–190.

Gibson, E.J. (1969). *Principles of perceptual learning and development*. New York: Appleton-Century-Crofts.

Glanzer, M. & Cunitz, A.R. (1966). Two storage mechanisms in free recall. *Journal of Verbal Learning and Verbal Behavior*, *5*, 351–360.

Golomb, C. (1973). Children's representation of the human figure: The effects of models, media, and instruction. *Genetic Psychology Monographs*, *87*, 197–251.

Golomb, C. (1981). Representation and reality: The origins and determinants of young children's drawings. *Review of Research in Visual Art Education*, *14*, 36–48.

Golomb, C. (1988). Symbolic inventions and transformations in child art. In K. Egan & D. Nadaner (Eds), *Imagination and education*. Milton Keynes: Open University Press.

Golomb, C. & Barr-Grossman, T. (1977). Representational development of the human figure in familial retardates. *Genetic Psychology Monographs*, *95*, 247–266.

Goodenough, F.L. (1926). *The measurement of intelligence by drawings*. New York: World Books.

Goodenough, F.L. & Harris, D.B. (1950). Studies in the psychology of children's drawings: II. 1928–1949. *Psychological Bulletin*, *47*, 369–433.

Goodnow, J. (1977). *Children's drawing*. London: Open Books.

Goodnow, J. (1978). Visible thinking: Cognitive aspects of change in drawings. *Child Development*, *49*, 637–641.

Goodnow, J.J., Wilkins, P., & Dawes, L. (1986). Acquiring cultural forms: Cognitive aspects of socialization illustrated by children's drawings and judgments of drawings. *International Journal of Behavioral Development*, *9*, 485–505.

Goodwin, J. (1982). Use of drawings in evaluating children who may be incest victims. *Children and Youth Services Review*, *4*, 269–278.

Granick, S. & Smith, L.J. (1953). Sex sequence in the Draw-A-Person test and its relation to the MMPI Masculinity–Femininity Scale. *Journal of Consulting Psychology*, *17*, 71–73.

Gray, D.M. & Pepitone, A. (1964). Effect of self-esteem on drawings of the human figure. *Journal of Consulting Psychology*, *28*, 452–455.

Gridley, P.F. (1938). Graphic representation of a man by four-year-old children in nine prescribed drawing situations. *Genetic Psychology Monographs*, *20*, 183–350.

Griffiths, R. (1945). *A study of imagination in early childhood and its function in mental development*. London: Kegan Paul, Trench, Trubner.

Guillaumin, J. (1961). Quelques faits et quelques réflexions à propos de l'orientation des profils humains dans les dessins d'enfants. *Enfance*, *14*, 57–75.

Haddon, A.C. (1904). Drawings by natives of British New Guinea. *Man*, *4*, 33–36.

Hammer, E.F. (1958). *The clinical application of projective drawings*. Springfield, IL: C.C. Thomas.

Harris, D.B. (1963). *Children's drawings as measures of intellectual maturity: A revision and extension of the Goodenough Draw-a-Man Test*. New York: Harcourt, Brace and World.

Harris, D.B. (1971). The case study. In G. Gensler (Ed.), *A report on preconference education research training programs for descriptive research in art education*. National Art Education Association.

Hartley, J.L., Somerville, S.C., von Cziesch Jensen, D., & Eliefja, C.C. (1982). Abstraction of individual styles from the drawings of five-year-old children. *Child Development*, *53*, 1193–1214.

Hathaway, S.R. & McKinley, J.C. (1940). A multiphasic personality schedule (Minnesota): I. Construction of the schedule. *Journal of Psychology*, *10*, 249–254.

Havighurst, R.J., Gunther, M.K., & Pratt, I.E. (1946). Environment and the Draw-a-Man test: The performance of Indian children. *Journal of Abnormal and Social Psychology*, *41*, 50–63.

Heinrich, P. & Triebe, J. (1972). Self-preferences in children's human figure drawings. *Journal of Personality Assessment*, *36*, 263–267.

Henderson, J.A. & Thomas, G.V. (1990). Looking ahead: Planning for the inclusion of detail affects relative sizes of head and trunk in children's human figure drawings. *British Journal of Developmental Psychology*, *8*, 383–391.

Hilger, M.I., Klett, W.G., & Watson, C.G. (1976). Performance of Ainu and Japanese six year olds on the Goodenough–Harris drawing test. *Perceptual and Motor Skills*, *42*, 435–438.

Hochberg, J. (1972). The representation of things and people. In E.H. Gombrich, J. Hochberg, & M. Black (Eds), *Art, perception and reality*. Baltimore, MD: Johns Hopkins University Press.

Howard, I.P. & Templeton, W.B. (1966). *Human spatial orientation*. London: John Wiley.

Hurlock, E.B. & Thomson, J.L. (1934). Children's drawings: An experimental study of perception. *Child Development*, *5*, 127–138.

Ingram, N. (1983). *Representation of three-dimensional spatial relationships on a two-dimensional picture surface*. Unpublished PhD thesis, University of Southampton.

Ingram, N. & Butterworth, G. (1989). The young child's representation of depth in drawing: Process and product. *Journal of Experimental Child Psychology*, *47*, 356–369.

Israelite, J. (1936). A comparison of the difficulty of items for intellectually normal children and mental defectives on the Goodenough drawing test. *American Journal of Orthopsychiatry*, *6*, 494–503.

Jolles, I. (1952). A study of the validity of some hypotheses for the qualitative interpretation of the H-T-P for children of elementary school age: I. Sexual identification. *Journal of Clinical Psychology*, *8*, 113–118.

Kahill, S. (1984). Human figure drawing in adults: An update of the empirical evidence, 1967–1982. *Canadian Psychology*, *25*, 269–292.

Karmiloff-Smith, A. (1986). From meta-processes to conscious access: Evidence from children's metalinguistic and repair data. *Cognition*, *23*, 95–147.

Karmiloff-Smith, A. (1990). Constraints on representational change: Evidence from children's drawing. *Cognition*, *34*, 57–83.

Kelley, S.J. (1985). The use of art therapy with the sexually-abused child. *Journal of Psychosocial Nursing and Mental Health Services*, *22*, 12–18.

Kellogg, R. (1969). *Analyzing children's art*. Palo Alto, CA: Mayfield.

Kennedy, J.M. (1983). What can we learn about pictures from the blind? *American Scientist*, *71*, 19–26.

Kerschensteiner, D.G. (1905). *Die Entwickelung der zeichnerischen Begabung*. Munich: Gerber.

Knopf, I. & Richards, T.W. (1952). The child's differentiation of sex as reflected in drawings of the human figure. *Journal of Genetic Psychology*, *81*, 99–112.

Koppitz, E.M. (1968). *Psychological evaluation of children's human figure drawings*. London: Grune and Stratton.

Laosa, L.M., Swartz, J.D., & Holtzman, W.H. (1973). Human figure drawings by normal children: A longitudinal study of perceptual-cognitive and personality development. *Developmental Psychology*, *8*, 350–356.

Lark-Horovitz, B., Barnhart, E.N., & Sills, E.M. (1939). *Graphic work-sample diagnosis: An analytical method of estimating children's drawing ability*. Cleveland, OH: Cleveland Museum of Art.

Lark-Horovitz, B., Lewis, H., & Luca, M. (1973). *Understanding children's art for better teaching*, 2nd edn. Columbus, OH: Charles E. Merrill.

Lobsien, M. (1905). Kinderzeichnung und Kunstkanon. *Zeitschrift für Pedagogische Psychologie*, *7*, 393–404.

Löwenfeld, V. (1939). *The nature of creative activity*. New York: Macmillan.

Löwenfeld, V. & Brittain, W.L. (1975). *Creative and mental growth*, 6th edn. London: Collier-Macmillan.

Luquet, G.H. (1913). *Les dessins d'un enfant*. Paris: Alcan.

Luquet, G.H. (1920). Les bonhommes têtards dans le dessin enfantin. *Journal de Psychologie Normale*, *17*, 684–710.

Luquet, G.H. (1927). *Le dessin enfantin*. Paris: Alcan.

Maccoby, E.E. (1968). What copying requires. *Ontario Journal of Educational Research*, *10*, 163–170.

Maccoby, E.E. & Bee, H.L. (1965). Some speculations concerning the lag between perceiving and performing. *Child Development*, *36*, 365–377.

Machover, K. (1949). *Personality projection in the drawings of the human figure*. Springfield, IL: C.C. Thomas.

Machover, K. (1951). Drawings of the human figure: A method of personality investigation. In H.H. Anderson & G.L. Anderson (Eds), *An introduction to projective techniques*. Englewood Cliffs, NJ: Prentice-Hall.

Maitland, L.M. (1895). What children draw to please themselves. *The Inland Educator*, *1*, 77–81.

Major, D.R. (1906). *First steps in mental growth*. New York: Macmillan.

Mann, B.S. & Lehman, E.B. (1976). Transparencies in children's human figure drawings: A developmental approach. *Studies in Art Education*, *18*, 41–48.

Marr, D. (1977). Analysis of occluding contour. *Proceedings of the Royal Society*, *B197*, 441–475.

Märtin, H. (1939). Die Motivwahl und ihr Wandel in der freien Zeichnung des Grundschulkindes. *Zeitschrift für Pedagogische Psychologie, 40*, 231–241.

Matthews, J. (1984). Children drawing: Are young children really scribbling? *Early Child Development and Care, 18*, 1–39.

McCarthy, D. (1944). A study of the reliability of the Goodenough Drawing Test of Intelligence. *Journal of Psychology, 18*, 201–216.

McCarty, S.A. (1924). *Children's drawings*. Baltimore, MD: Williams and Wilkins.

McCurdy, H.G. (1947). Group and individual variability on the Goodenough Draw-a-Person test. *Journal of Educational Psychology, 38*, 428–436.

McElwee, E.W. (1932). The reliability of the Goodenough intelligence test used with subnormal children fourteen years of age. *Journal of Applied Psychology, 16*, 217–218.

McElwee, E.W. (1934). Profile drawings of normal and subnormal children. *Journal of Applied Psychology, 18*, 599–603.

McHugh, A. (1963). H-T-P proportion and perspective in Negro, Puerto Rican and white children. *Journal of Clinical Psychology, 19*, 312–314.

Millar, S. (1975). Visual experience or translation rules? Drawing the human figure by blind and sighted children. *Perception, 4*, 363–371.

Moore, V. (1986). The use of a colouring task to elucidate children's drawings of a solid cube. *British Journal of Developmental Psychology, 4*, 335–340.

Mott, S.M. (1954). Concept of mother: A study of four- and five-year-old children. *Child Development, 25*, 99–106.

Munn, N. (1973). *Walbiri iconography: Graphic representation and cultural symbolism in a central Australian society*. New York: Cornell University Press.

Murphy, M.M. (1957). Sexual differentiation of male and female job applicants on the DAP test. *Journal of Clinical Psychology, 13*, 87–88.

Nash, H. & Harris, D.B. (1970). Body proportions in children's drawings of a man. *Journal of Genetic Psychology, 117*, 85–90.

O'Keefe, R., Leskovsky, K., O'Brien, L., Yater, S.S., & Barklay, M.W. (1971). Influences of age, sex and ethnic origin on the Goodenough–Harris drawing test performance by disadvantaged preschool children. *Perceptual and Motor Skills, 33*, 708–710.

Olivier, F. (1974). Le dessin enfantin, est-il une ecriture? *Enfance, 3*, 183–216.

Olson, D.R. & Bialystock, E. (1983). *Spatial cognition: The structure and development of mental representations of spatial relations*. Hillsdale, NJ: Lawrence Erlbaum Associates Inc.

Opie, I. & Opie, P. (1969). *Children's games in street and playground*. Oxford: Oxford University Press.

Paget, G.W. (1932). Some drawings of men and women made by children of certain non-European races. *Journal of the Royal Anthropological Institute, 62*, 127–144.

Papadakis-Michaelides, E.A. (1989). *Development of children's drawings in relation to gender and culture*. Unpublished PhD thesis, University of Birmingham.

Partridge, L. (1902). Children's drawings of men and women. *Studies in Education, 2*, 163–179.

Pfeffer, K. (1984). Interpretation of studies of ethnic identity: Draw-a-person as a measure of ethnic identity. *Perceptual and Motor Skills, 59*, 835–838.

Piaget, J. (1950). *The psychology of intelligence*. London: Routledge and Kegan Paul.

Piaget, J. (1953). *The origin of intelligence in the child*. London: Routledge and Kegan Paul.

Piaget, J. & Inhelder, B. (1956). *The child's conception of space*. London: Routledge and Kegan Paul.

Piaget, J. & Inhelder, B. (1969). *The psychology of the child*. London: Routledge and Kegan Paul.

Pollak, J.M. (1986). Human figure-drawing performance of LD children: Research and clinical perspectives. *Learning Disability Quarterly*, *9*, 173–181.

Probst, M. (1906). Les dessins des enfants Kabyles. *Archives de Psychologie*, *6*, 131–140.

Prytula, R.E. & Thompson, N.D. (1973). Analysis of emotional indicators in human figure drawings as related to self-esteem. *Perceptual and Motor Skills*, *37*, 795–802.

Raven, J., Raven, J.C., & Court, J.H. (1991). *Manual for Raven's Progressive Matrices and Vocabulary Scales*. Oxford: Oxford Psychologists Press.

Reith, E. (1988). The development of use of contour lines in children's drawings of figurative and non-figurative three-dimensional models. *Archives de Psychologie*, *56*, 83–103.

Reuning, H. & Wortley, W. (1973). Psychological studies of the Bushmen. *Psychologia Africana Monograph Supplement*, No. 7.

Ricci, C. (1887). *L'Arte dei Bambini*. Bologna: N. Zanichelli.

Richards, M. & Ross, H. (1967). Developmental changes in children's drawings. *British Journal of Educational Psychology*, *37*, 73–80.

Roback, H.B. (1968). Human figure drawings: Their utility in the clinical psychologist's armamentarium for personality assessment. *Psychological Bulletin*, *70*, 1–19.

Rosen, A. & Boe, E. (1968). Frequency of nude figure drawings. *Journal of Projective Technique and Personality Assessment*, *32*, 483–485.

Rosenberg, M. (1965). *Society and the adolescent self-image*. Princeton, NJ: Princeton University Press.

Rouma, G. (1913). *Le language graphique de l'enfant*. Paris: Misch et Thron.

Schildkrout, M.S., Shenker, I.R., & Sonnenblick, M. (1972). *Human figure drawings in adolescence*. New York: Brunner Mazel.

Schubert, A. (1930). Drawings of Orotchen children and young people. *Pedagogical Seminary*, *37*, 232–243.

Schuyten, M.C. (1904). De oorspronkelijke "Ventjes" der Antwerpsch Schoolkindern. *Paedologisch Jaarboek*, *5*, 1–87.

Scott, L.H. (1981). Measuring intelligence with the Goodenough-Harris drawing test. *Psychological Bulletin*, *89*, 483–505.

Sechrest, L. & Wallace, J. (1964). Figure drawings and naturally occurring events: Elimination of the expansive euphoria hypothesis. *Journal of Educational Psychology*, *53*, 42–44.

Selfe, L. (1983). *Normal and anomalous representational drawing ability in children*. London: Academic Press.

Sinha, M. (1971). Draw a man test scores of British and non-British children. *Indian Educational Review*, *6*, 79–87.

Sitton, R. & Light, P. (1992). Drawing to differentiate: Flexibility in young children's human figure drawings. *British Journal of Developmental Psychology*, *10*, 25–33.

Solley, C.M. & Haigh, G. (1957). A note to Santa Claus. *Topeka Research Papers, The Menninger Foundation*, *18*, 4–5.

Spensley, F. (1990). Representational redescription and children's drawings. Paper presented at the *British Psychological Society Cognitive Psychology Section Annual Conference*, University of Leicester, September.

Spoerl, D.T. (1940). The drawing ability of mentally retarded children. *Journal of Genetic Psychology*, *57*, 259–277.

Stratford, B. & Mei Lan Au (1988). The development of drawing in Chinese and English children. *Early Child Development and Care*, *30*, 141–165.

Swensen, C.H. (1955). Sexual differentiation on the Draw-a-Person test. *Journal of Clinical Psychology*, *11*, 37–40.

Swensen, C.H. (1957). Empirical evaluations of human figure drawings. *Psychological Bulletin*, *54*, 431–466.

Swensen, C.H. (1968). Empirical evaluations of human figure drawings: 1957–1966. *Psychological Bulletin, 70,* 20–44.

Swensen, C.H. & Newton, K.R. (1955). Development of sexual differentiation on the Draw-a-Person test. *Journal of Clinical Psychology, 11,* 417–419.

Taylor, M. & Bacharach, V.R. (1981). The development of drawing rules: Metaknowledge about drawing influences performance on nondrawing tasks. *Child Development, 52,* 373–375.

Terman, L.M. (1916). *The measurement of intelligence.* Boston, MA: Houghton Mifflin.

Terman, L.M. & Merrill, M.A. (1960). *Stanford-Binet Intelligence Scale.* Boston, MA: Houghton Mifflin.

Thomas, G.V. & Gray, R. (1992). Children's drawings of topics differing in emotional significance: Effects on placement relative to a self drawing. *Journal of Child Psychology and Psychiatry, 33,* 1097–1104.

Thomas, G.V. & Tsalimi, A. (1988). Effects of order of drawing head and trunk on their relative sizes in children's human figure drawings. *British Journal of Developmental Psychology, 6,* 191–203.

Thomas, G.V., Chaigne, E., & Fox, T.J. (1989). Children's drawings of topics differing in significance: Effects on size of drawing. *British Journal of Developmental Psychology, 7,* 321–331.

Tolor, A. & Tolor, B. (1955). Judgement of children's popularity from their human figure drawings. *Journal of Projective Techniques, 19,* 170–176.

Tolor, A. & Tolor, B. (1974). Children's figure drawings and changing attitudes towards sex roles. *Psychological Reports, 34,* 343–349.

Vygotsky, L.S. (1978). *Mind in society.* Cambridge, MA: Harvard University Press.

Wales, R. (1990). Children's pictures. In R. Grieve & M. Hughes (Eds), *Understanding children.* Oxford: Blackwell.

Wallach, M.A. & Leggett, M.I. (1972). Testing the hypothesis that a person will be consistent: Stylistic consistency versus situational specificity in size of children's drawings. *Journal of Personality, 40,* 309–330.

Wechsler, D. (1967). *Manual for the Wechsler Preschool and Primary Scale of Intelligence.* New York: Psychological Corporation.

Wechsler, D. (1974). *Manual for the Wechsler Intelligence Scale for Children,* Revised edn. New York: Psychological Corporation.

Weider, A. & Noller, P.A. (1950). Objective studies of children's drawings of human figures: I. Sex awareness and socio-economic level. *Journal of Clinical Psychology, 6,* 319–325.

Weider, A. & Noller, P.A. (1953). Objective studies of children's drawings of human figures: II. Sex, age, intelligence. *Journal of Clinical Psychology, 9,* 20–23.

Werner, H. (1948). *Comparative psychology of mental development.* Chicago, IL: Follett.

Willats, J. (1985). Drawings systems revisited: The complementary roles of projection systems and denotation systems in the analysis of children's drawings. In N.H. Freeman & M.V. Cox (Eds), *Visual order: The nature and development of pictorial representation.* Cambridge: Cambridge University Press.

Willats, J. (1987). Marr and pictures: An information-processing account of children's drawings. *Archives de Psychologie, 55,* 105–125.

Willatts, P. & Dougal, S. (n.d.). *Planning ahead: Influence of figure orientation on size of head in children's drawings of a man.* Unpublished manuscript, University of Dundee.

Williams, J.H. (1935). Validity and reliability of the Goodenough intelligence test. *School and Society, 41,* 653–656.

Willsdon, J.A. (1977). A discussion of some sex differences in a study of human figure drawings by children aged four-and-a-half to seven-and-a-half years. In G. Butterworth (Ed.), *The child's representation of the world.* New York: Plenum Press.

Wilson, B. (1985). The artistic tower of Babel: Inextricable links between culture and graphic development. *Visual Arts Research*, *11*, 90–104.

Wilson, B. & Wilson, M. (1984). Children's drawings in Egypt: Cultural style acquisition as graphic development. *Visual Arts Research*, *10*, 13–26.

Winner, E. (1989). How can Chinese children draw so well? *Journal of Aesthetic Education*, *23*, 41–63.

Wohl, A. & Kaufman, B. (1985). *Silent screams and hidden cries: An interpretation of artwork by children from violent homes*. New York: Brunner Mazel.

Wolf, D. & Perry, M.D. (1988). From endpoints to repertoires: Some new conclusions about drawing development. *Journal of Aesthetic Education*, *22*, 17–34.

Wolff, W. (1946). *The personality of the pre-school child*. New York: Grune and Stratton.

Yates, A., Beutler, L.E., & Crago, M. (1985). Drawings by child victims of incest. *Child Abuse and Neglect*, *9*, 183–189.

Yepsen, T.N. (1929). The reliability of the Goodenough Drawing Test with feeble-minded subjects. *Journal of Educational Psychology*, *20*, 448–451.

Zaporozhets, A.V. (1965). The development of perception in the preschool child. In P.H. Mussen (Ed.), European research in cognitive development. *Monograph of the Society for Research in Child Development*, *30* (serial no. 100), 82–102.

Author Index

147

Subject Index

Other Titles in the Series
Essays in Developmental Psychology
Series Editors: Peter Bryant, George Butterworth, Harry McGurk

KNOWING CHILDREN

Experiments in Conversation and Cognition

MICHAEL SIEGAL (University of Queensland)

It has been often maintained that young children's knowledge is limited to perceptual appearances; in this "preoperational" stage of development, there are profound conceptual limitations in that they have little understanding of numerical and causal relations and are incapable of insight into the minds of others. Their apparent inability to perform well on traditional developmental measures has led researchers to accept a model of the young child as plagued by conceptual deficits. These ideas have had a major impact on educational programs. Many have either accepted the view that the young are not ready for instruction, especially in subjects such as mathematics and science.

However, this essay provides evidence that children's stage-like performance on the many tasks that have been used to demonstrate their limitations can be reinterpreted in terms of the language used in experiments. In many specialized experimental settings, children may inadvertently perceive adults' well-meaning questions as redundant, insincere, irrelevant, uninformative, or ambiguous. Under these conditions, there is a clash between the conversational worlds of children and adults. Children do not share an experimenter's purpose in questioning and how his or her words are intended. They do not disclose the depth of their understanding and may respond to an experimenter's questions incorrectly even when they are certain of the right answer.

In this light, a different model of development emerges. It proposes that young children have abstract knowledge that can be examined through attention to their conversational experience. The implications for instruction in subjects such as mathematics and science are significant.

0-86377-158-0 1991 154pp. $31.95 £19.95 hbk. / 0-86377-159-9 $15.95 £8.95 pbk.

For UK/Europe, please send orders to: *Lawrence Erlbaum Associates Ltd., Mail Order Department, 27 Church Road, Hove, East Sussex, BN3 2FA, England. Note, prices shown here are correct at time of going to press, but may change. Prices outside Europe may differ from those shown.* **Please send USA & Canadian orders to:** *Lawrence Erlbaum Associates Inc., 365 Broadway, Hillsdale, New Jersey, NJ07642, USA.*

PHONOLOGICAL SKILLS AND LEARNING TO READ

USHA GOSWAMI, (Cambridge University)
PETER BRYANT, (Oxford University)

"Goswami and Bryant assemble an impressive number of research studies which bear on their thesis, outlining them clearly and succinctly. They write persuasively but never dogmatically, revealing a refreshing willingness to give credit to theoretical positions other than their own. This book deserves serious attention by all those who are keen to relate the practice of the teaching of reading to theory which is firmly grounded in careful empirical work." **Katherine Perera,** (The Times Higher Education Supplement).

"I think this is an excellent and timely book. It has been a pleasure reviewing it." **Dr Charles Hulme** (Reader in Psychology, University of York)

This book sets out to integrate recent exciting research on the precursors of reading and early reading strategies adopted by children in the classroom. It aims to develop a theory about why early phonological skills are crucial in learning to read, and shows how phonological knowledge about rhymes and other units of sound helps children learn about letter sequences when beginning to be taught to read. The authors begin by contrasting theories which suggest that children's phonological awareness is a result of the experience of learning to read and those that suggest that phonological awareness precedes, and is a causal determinant of, reading. The authors argue for a version of the second kind of theory and show that children are aware of speech units, called onset and rime, before they learn to read and spell. An important part of the argument is that children make analogies and inferences about these letter sequences in order to read and write new words.

Contents: Preface. Phonological Awareness and Reading. How Children Read Words. Spelling and Phonological Awareness. How Children Read and Write New Words. Comparisons with Backward Readers and Spellers.Correlations and Longitudinal Predictions. Teaching Children About Sounds. Do Children Read (And Fail to Learn to Read) in Different Ways From Each Other? Theories About Learning to Read.

0-86377-150-5 1990 160pp. $31.95 £19.95 hb / 0-86377-151-3 $13.95 £8.95 pb

For UK/Europe, please send orders to: Lawrence Erlbaum Associates Ltd., Mail Order Department, 27 Church Road, Hove, East Sussex, BN3 2FA, England. Note, prices shown here are correct at time of going to press, but may change. Prices outside Europe may differ from those shown. Please send USA & Canadian orders to: Lawrence Erlbaum Associates Inc., 365 Broadway, Hillsdale, New Jersey, NJ07642, USA.

Titles in the Series
Essays in Developmental Psychology
Series Editors: Peter Bryant, George Butterworth, Harry McGurk

PUBLISHED TITLES

Cox: Children's Drawings of the Human Figure

0-86377-268-4 1993 168pp. $36.95 £19.95 HB

Forrester: The Development of Young Children's Social-Cognitive Skills

0-86377-232-3 1992 216pp. $37.50 £19.95 HB

Garton: Social Interaction and the Development of Language and Cognition

0-86377-227-7 1992 168pp. $37.50 £19.95 HB

Goodnow/Collins: Development According to Parents: The Nature, Sources and Consequences of Parents' Ideas

0-86377-160-2 1990 200pp. $31.95 £19.95 HB / 0-86377-161-0 $15.95 £8.95 PB

Goswami: Analogical Reasoning in Children

0-86377-226-9 1992 156pp. $28.50 £14.95 HB

Goswami/Bryant: Phonological Skills and Learning to Read

0-86377-150-5 1990 174pp. $33.95 £19.95 HB / 0-86377-151-3 $16.95 £8.95 PB

Harris: Language Experience and Early Language Development: From Input to Uptake

0-86377-231-5 1992 160pp. $35.95 £19.95 HB / 0-86377-238-2 $16.50 £8.95 PB

Siegal: Knowing Children: Experiments in Conversation and Cognition

0-86377-158-0 1991 128pp. $31.95 £19.95 HB / 0-86377-159-9 $14.50 £7.95 PB

Smith: Necessary Knowledge: Piagetian Perspectives on Constructivism

0-86377-270-6 1993 256pp. $46.50 £24.95 HB

Sonuga-Barke/Webley: Children's Saving: A Study in the Development of Economic Behaviour

0-86377-233-1 1993 168pp. $28.50 £14.95 HB

For UK/Europe, please send orders to: Lawrence Erlbaum Associates Ltd., Mail Order Department, 27 Church Road, Hove, East Sussex, BN3 2FA, England. Note, prices shown here are correct at time of going to press, but may change. Prices outside Europe may differ from those shown. Please send USA & Canadian orders to: Lawrence Erlbaum Associates Inc., 365 Broadway, Hillsdale, New Jersey, NJ07642, USA.

DATE DUE